Contents

For Antony and Claire Winn

I wish to acknowledge the invaluable contribution made by Pat, my wife, in the preparation of this work.

Introduction

GCSE course: British social and economic history

Questions of Evidence: Britain since 1700 has been written and designed to help you achieve success in your history course. In learning about the making of modern Britain you will be studying a wide range of topics and key issues which will give you a detailed picture of the main changes that have taken place during the last two hundred years.

At the same time you will be learning about the methods that historians use to help them find out about the past. In doing so you will come across words and phrases which may be unfamiliar. These words and phrases may well appear in the examination papers, and you may be expected to use them in your answers. Thus it is useful for you to have a working knowledge of the **terms** which are used by historians, and which are introduced and explained in the following sections. You will also have opportunities to practise some of the skills of the historian, in ways that will enable you to increase your own knowledge and understanding of the recent history of Britain. One of the ways in which you can learn about the past is by studying historical sources.

What are historical sources?

The raw material of history is found in **sources** which have survived from the past. A source is anything that provides information for a historian to use. The knowledge and skills of the historian are acquired mainly by understanding and using source materials. Historians obtain information from various sources and in many ways:

- they study and examine written extracts of all kinds, illustrations and maps;
- they listen to oral sources (for example people talking about their memories of the past) either directly from the person/s concerned or through recordings;
- they examine historical objects (known as artefacts) which have survived from the past;
- they look at, and study, buildings and the landscape;
- they read books and articles written by other historians;
- they study media programmes (radio, film, television) on history.

The historical sources in this book have been selected to cover the main topics in courses of British Social and Economic History and to provide many varied examples of written, statistical and picture sources for you to work with. You will perhaps gain experience of some of the other sources mentioned above by visiting historical sites and museums, from film, television and radio programmes, and by talking to people about their memories of the past. When working with a source it is useful to establish its **form** and its **type**.

Sources: forms
The wide variety of historical sources in this book take many different forms. The written forms include documentary source extracts of all kinds: books (including textbooks), newspapers, pamphlets, Acts of Parliament, official records produced by Parliament and government, personal or private writings, letters, statistics and tables. The picture sources also take many different forms: drawings, engravings, cartoons, photographs, maps and diagrams. In comparing different forms of sources (for example, a drawing is very different from a photograph) it will become clear that each *form* of source will also present different problems for the historian. Establishing the form of a source, and being able to compare the main features of two or more forms of sources are important and useful historical skills. As well as comparing different forms of sources, historians also study different types of sources.

Sources: types
Sources are often classed as being of two main types: **primary sources** and **secondary sources**.

Primary source A primary source is usually one which was produced (written, drawn, photographed, spoken) at the time that the event it describes occurred, or during the period being studied. For example, if a historian is studying the part played by women in the First World War then posters designed to encourage women to work in munitions (armaments) factories, the uniform of a nurse who served in a military hospital and the diary of a suffragette, would all be primary sources. A primary source can also be produced after the event described or the period being studied by someone who was there or involved at the time. Thus, if a woman wrote about her memories of the war many years after the war had ended, it would also be a primary source.

Secondary source A secondary source is one which was produced later than the event or period being studied, by people who were not present at the time or who were not involved in the events described. For example a book or article written by an historian today about the role of women in the First World War, or a school textbook which included a chapter on that topic, would be classed as secondary sources. The information in a secondary source has usually been obtained from other primary and secondary sources. It is important to ask whether the author or producer of a secondary source has read and used other relevant primary and secondary sources in his/her work.

Note: It is not always possible to be certain when deciding whether a source is primary or secondary, for much depends on the use to which the source is to be put. You cannot really decide whether a source is primary or secondary until you know what it is that you are trying to find out about. Even experienced historians may *sometimes* have difficulty in deciding whether a particular source is primary or secondary. It is also important to decide the **validity** and **reliability** of any source you are intending to use.

Validity A source is said to have validity if it can provide convincing evidence to help in answering questions about the event or period of history being studied. Before asking detailed questions of a particular source it is important to decide whether it will be useful in providing evidence for your enquiries. Thus a particular source may be valid and provide evidence for the study of one topic but may not be valid for another topic.

Reliability When using a source it is important to decide its reliability, that is how genuine (authentic), accurate or truthful it is. It is also important to realise that primary sources are *not* *necessarily* more useful and more reliable than secondary sources simply because they are primary. You should not fall into the trap of thinking that because a source is primary it *must* be reliable and useful in the study of a particular topic in history. A particular source may be reliable in answering some questions, but of no use in answering other questions. In other words, a source can sometimes be both reliable and unreliable. You may wish to ask the following questions about a source to establish its reliability:

- What is the **form** of the source?
- What **type** of source is it?
- Is the source true?
- Is it a copy?
- Could it be a fake?
- Where did the source come from?
- Who produced the source?
- Why and how was the source produced?
- When was the source produced?
- How old is the source?

In working through the book you will be expected to assess the **validity** and **reliability** of the selected sources. You will also have opportunities to use the sources to obtain evidence and to show what you know, what you understand, and what you can do.

Using historical sources to provide evidence
In a courtroom, a lawyer questions the witness in the witness box in order to obtain evidence which can be used to try and establish the truth of the case being heard. Similarly by asking questions of historical sources it is possible to obtain **evidence** which can be used to try and establish what happened in the past, why it happened, what resulted from the event, and how it affected those living at the time. Thus the historical sources in this book are accompanied by a full range of questions which will help you to observe, record, analyze, interpret and understand historical evidence.

The lawyer in the courtroom may decide to examine other witnesses in order to provide further evidence, which may agree with (i.e. confirm or support) or disagree with (i.e. oppose or differ from) the evidence already obtained. In a similar way, a historian may wish to examine other sources before making up his/her mind or before reaching conclusions about what happened in the past. Thus the last section of questions on each topic is designed to link sources and to link evidence. By linking evidence from different sources you will begin to realise that the evidence obtained by questioning one historical source can be opened up and developed by using other sources. However, just as the lawyer sometimes finds that a witness may be unreliable or untruthful, so may the historian find that some historical sources present problems.

Some problems in the use of historical sources

As you work through this book you may experience some of the problems which historians themselves face when working with sources. For example, you will find that some of the sources are incomplete and may only give the viewpoint of one individual or one group of people. Therefore the evidence and the conclusions you reach may also be incomplete, or *inconclusive*. If more, or different, sources were available the conclusions reached might be very different. You will also begin to realise that some kinds of sources may be more reliable than others, or that two or more sources, which appear to be equally reliable, provide *contradictory* evidence (i.e. one source provides evidence which contradicts or disagrees with the evidence in another source). How do you decide which source is the more reliable or which evidence is the most accurate?

As you work with sources, you will begin to realise that the judgements you make or the conclusions you reach may be very different from those of other course members. It will also be clear that the conclusions reached or statements you make are not fixed or final. Such conclusions, or historical judgements, although formed from evidence, are called **provisional statements**. Thus some of the source material and questions in this book will enable you to understand that a study of history does not always produce a set of correct or final answers.

The sources have also been selected, linked and arranged so as to help you understand a number of key ideas or **concepts** which are used by historians in their study of the past.

Concepts

Bias

A biased source is one that gives a one-sided or unbalanced view or provides 'selected' information. An important skill for the historian is the ability to detect possible bias in the sources being studied. 'Taking sides' or partiality occurs in many historical sources, and a degree of 'unconscious' or 'natural' bias may also be present. Thus most sources are likely to be biased to some extent. Just because a source is biased does not mean that it is no use to an historian. However, a historian needs to be aware of the ways in which bias can occur. For example:

- certain facts or information may be deliberately included or left out;
- particular attention may be drawn to some information by the use of 'loaded' words or phrases;
- a written source may include a general statement (**generalization**) based on little or no information;
- a cartoon may caricature individuals unfairly and use emotional language;
- information may be deliberately included which is intended to promote or damage a cause or interest (known as **propaganda**);
- a judgement may be made, or views or opinions expressed, based on insufficient or inaccurate information (known as **prejudice**);
- a source may have been deliberately altered or changed at a later date.

It is important to be aware of the possibility of bias when using sources and to be able to detect instances of bias. Thus the historian needs to consider the viewpoint and motive of the person or group who produced the source. For example, is the person who produced the source involved with a particular cause or movement which might make the source biased? It is also important to ask whether the writer or producer of an historical source had access to accurate information at the time. Recognizing the difference between **fact** and **opinion** is essential in detecting bias in a source. When examining long statements it is worth considering the balance between fact and opinion. Thus some of the questions in this book ask you to show that you know the difference between **fact** and **opinion**.

Example

Jethro Tull's book *Horse Hoeing Husbandry* was first published in 1733 (**fact**). *Horse Hoeing Husbandry* was the most important book on farming published in the eighteenth century (**opinion**).

Note: It is not *always* possible to make a definite distinction between fact and opinion. Bias may influence a writer's reporting of the facts and may be the cause of the partisan recording of fact, or of confusing fact and opinion.

Similarities and differences

Perhaps you have at sometimes attempted 'spot the difference' competitions which appear in comics, magazines and newspapers. The historian uses a similar skill when comparing two or more sources. Identifying and understanding **similarities** (features which are alike) and **differences** (features which are unlike) are important concepts in the study of history. People, events, issues and institutions may be compared and contrasted by asking: What is different? What is the same? Sometimes it may be appropriate to use this process to link activities in the past with the present. This may enable current situations to be interpreted in an historical context. You will have opportunities to compare and contrast, and record similarities and differences when examining many of the sources selected for this book.

Continuity and change

When studying the past it is important to understand that some things remained the same or developed without interruption (**continuity**); while others altered or one thing was replaced by another (**change**). It is also important to recognize that the pace or rate at which change takes place can vary and is not always 'progressive', 'consistent or constant (even and steady). For example, population has had periods of slow growth and periods of rapid growth; and developments in technology have experienced sudden bursts of activity and rapid change. Concepts such as continuity and change can help us to become aware that the past (then) is different from the present (now). It can also help us to realise that we share certain characteristics and values with people and situations in the past.

Causes and consequence (effect)

Having observed and recorded similarities and differences, continuities and changes, historians try to explain why things happened in the way they did (**causes**) and what the effects or results were (**consequences**). That is, they try to explain the events of the past. A study of history shows that there were usually a number of reasons or causes for a changing situation, some of which were *immediate* causes (the occasion) of

an event; others of which were short term causes; and others which were long term. Similarly, when studying the consequences of events or changes in history you will realise that they usually involve more than one result or effect. It is important to know the difference between the causes of an event or change and the effects that resulted from them. Thus some of the questions in this book are designed to give you practice in distinguishing between cause and consequence.

Motivation

History is concerned with people, and it is important to understand that an individual, or a group of people can make things happen, and can influence the course of history so that things sometimes turned out differently from what might have been expected, or from what was intended. Therefore it is important to look for the reasons why individuals or groups in history took certain actions when they did, and to try to understand their **motives** (reasons for doing so).

Empathy

Historians are interested in trying to understand how people in the past thought, believed or felt. This understanding is known as **empathy**. You might describe it, in simple terms, as 'putting yourself in somebody else's shoes', that is trying to perceive (see and understand) historical events and situations as those living at the time might have seen them. When attempting to empathise with people in the past and to recreate historical situations it is essential to know all that you can about them, the period they lived in, and the events which took place at that time. This knowledge can be interpreted through imagination to increase understanding of how people in the past thought and felt, and of why and how they acted and reacted as they did to particular happenings or circumstances. This may enable you to explain why things happened as they did. It is also important to recognize that people in the past (as they do today) often differed from each other in the way they perceived events or situations. For example, a millowner might not feel the same way as a factory reformer about the use of child labour. It is also important to consider how the experiences of individuals or groups of people in the past might have affected their feelings or attitudes. Thus some of the questions in this book will ask you to **empathise** with people and events. You will need to base your answers on the sources and evidence available, and use your imagination in interpreting them. In writing an empathetic account, you should try to avoid anachronisms – that is, the inclusion of information which could not have been known at the time.

Communication

In answering questions and presenting information, it is important that you communicate clearly and accurately, making correct and appropriate use of historical terms, and that you can construct a logical argument, ranging from narrative to empathetic understanding. The questions accompanying the sources in each topic or chapter require responses in a variety of forms. Some of the questions ask for answers in continuous prose (essay form); others are objective or short answer questions; and some structured questions are also included. The last section of questions in each topic is designed to provide opportunities to link sources and evidence. In presenting answers, there are opportunities to identify, interpret, analyze, record, comprehend, evaluate, extract, select, arrange, hypothesise, compare and make judgements on historical sources. Written answers may involve argument, description, the creation of a list, or translating from one form to another – for example, by explaining a table or chart; or by putting written information into graph form. When examining a source for evidence, it is important for you to be able to distinguish between the more significant facts and features and those which are less so. Although some of your answers are likely to be simply descriptive, remember that you are more likely to gain higher marks if you can refer to why the source was produced and to the possible attitudes of those who produced it.

Beyond GCSE

Working through *Questions of Evidence: Britain since 1700* should help you to understand the main features of the economic and social history of modern Britain. It is hoped that the book will also stimulate your interest and enthusiasm for the study of the past, and provide a sound basis for further study and the pursuit of your personal interests.

1 The agricultural pioneers

A Extract from 'Horse Hoeing Husbandry' by Jethro Tull, published in 1733.

"When I sowed turnips by hand, and hoed them with a hand hoe, the expence was great, and the operation not half performed, by the deceitfulness of the hoers, who left half the land unhoed . . . and then the grass and weeds grew the faster. . . . In the new method they [the turnips] are more certain to come up quickly; because in every row half the seed is planted about four inches deep, and the other half is planted exactly over that, at the depth of half an inch, falling in after the earth has covered the first half. Thus planted, let the weather be never so dry, the deeper seed will come up; but if it raineth (immediately after planting) the shallow will come up first. . . . Drilled turnips, by being nowhere but in the rows, may be more easily seen than those which come up at random . . . it is very rarely that a . . . weed comes up in the same line amongst them . . . we know that whatever comes up in the interval is not a turnip."

B Description of farming in Norfolk from 'The Farmer's Tour' by Arthur Young, published in 1771.

" . . . great improvements have been made by means of the following circumstances: *First* By inclosing without the assistance of Parliament. *Second* By a spirited use of marl and clay. *Third* By the introduction of an excellent course of crops. *Fourth* By the culture of turnips well hoed. *Fifth* By the culture of clover and rye-grass. *Sixth* By landlords granting long leases. *Seventh* By the country being divided chiefly into large farms.

Still the whole success of the undertaking depends on this point: No fortune will be made in Norfolk by farming unless a judicious course of crops be pursued. That which has been chiefly adopted by the Norfolk farmers is: 1 Turnips, 2 Barley, 3 Clover: or clover and rye-grass, 4 Wheat.

. . . no small farmers could effect such great changes as have been done in Norfolk. . . ."

C Thomas Coke inspecting sheep on his farm at Holkham in Norfolk.

> **D** **Extract from 'Thoughts on England'**
> **by Francois de la Rochefoucauld.**
> "... Mr Bakewell ... a farmer ...
> began by buying every kind of animal, the
> best specimens he could find, and by
> crossing them he has achieved a breed
> which preserves all the good qualities and
> excellence ... without any of their
> defects. ... After many ... attempts ...
> Mr Bakewell has achieved the finest breed
> of carthorses, of cows, of sheep, of pigs and
> so on. ... His sheep have the finest wool
> combined with such a carcase as those
> which produce fine wool seldom have. ...
> They have also the advantage of fattening
> more quickly. Lastly his pigs are large,
> with big bellies and very large legs; they
> fatten very well on potatoes, which other
> pigs do not. They also get fat in a short
> time."

Questions

1 *Read Source* A .
  a Is this a primary or a secondary source? Give reasons for your answer.
  b What were the disadvantages of sowing and of hoeing turnips by hand?
  c What were the benefits of planting seed by the 'new method'?
  d Jethro Tull invented a horse-drawn seed-drill which sowed seeds in rows at a regular depth
  and a horse-drawn hoe which penetrated deeper into the ground. If you had been living in the
  eighteenth century would you have: (i) used these new inventions; (ii) continued the old
  methods; or (iii) looked for more information? Give reasons for your answer.

2 *Read Source* B .
  a What farming changes had taken place in Norfolk in the eighteenth century?
  b Which of the seven reasons for improvement did Arthur Young believe the most important?
  c Why might the willingness of landowners to grant long leases (up to 21 years) encourage
  tenant farmers to improve the land and to introduce new farming methods?
  d Is Arthur Young writing mainly about *short-term* or *long-term* factors for improvements?
  e Why is the evidence of Arthur Young important to historians?

3 *Look at Source* C .
  a Thomas Coke of Holkham in Norfolk was a great landowner and famous farmer. How has the
  artist made Coke the most important figure in the painting?
  b Did Coke look after the sheep himself? How do you know?
  c What is the background and setting for the painting? Can you suggest why this was chosen?
  d For what purpose do you think this picture might have been painted? Explain your answer.
  e Coke held annual 'sheep shearings' which attracted visitors from home and abroad. How
  might such gatherings help to spread new methods of farming?

4 *Read Source* D .
  a What was the occupation of Robert Bakewell and for what was he famous?
  b By what means did he succeed in raising the finest breeds of animals?
  c The animals bred by Bakewell were large and fattened quickly. Why was this an advantage
  for animal breeders and farmers?

Linking evidence

5 Sources A , B , C and D have a common theme. What is it?

6 In what ways do the Sources provide evidence to suggest that larger farms and longer leases
encouraged improved farming methods?

2.1 Enclosing the commons

'Enclosure' was the re-organizing of the land into compact farms whose fields were enclosed by hedges.

A **Extract from 'Reasons For and Against Enclosing Open Fields' by Stephen Addington, published in 1772.**
"The cottagers have little parcels of land in the ploughed fields, with commons rights for a cow and three or four sheep, by the assistance of which, and with the profits of a little trade or their daily labour, they procure a very comfortable living. Their ploughed land furnishes them with wheat and barley for bread, and, in many places, with beans or peas to feed a hog or two for meat; with the straw they thatch their cottage, and winter their cow, which gives a breakfast and supper of milk, nine or ten months in the year. They have likewise a right to cut turf, roots and furze on the common, which must be a great advantage to those who have not money to purchase other fuel."

B **(i) Map showing the village of Strettington in the eighteenth century.**

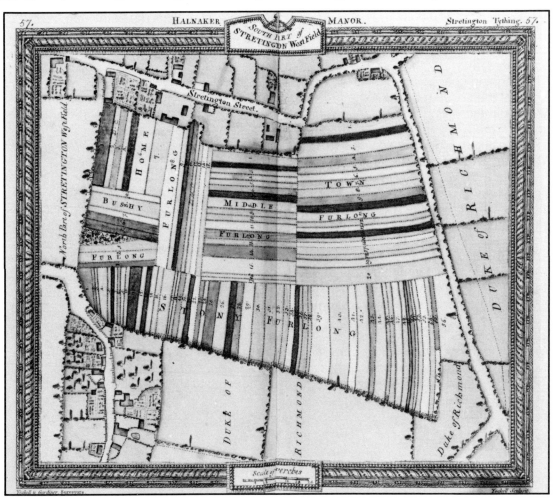

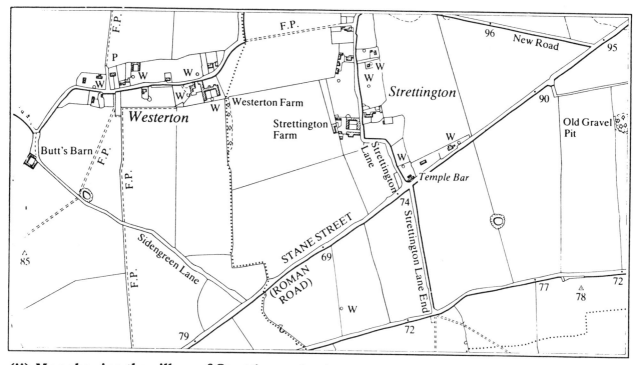

(ii) Map showing the village of Strettington in the nineteenth century.

Questions

1 *Read Source* A .
  a Does this Source describe the system of farming under: (i) the open field system; or (ii) the system of enclosure?
  b What advantages did this system of farming have for the cottagers?
  c How did the common land of the village provide for many of the cottagers' needs?

2 *Look at Sources* B (i) *and* B (ii).
  a Which of the two maps is the earliest?
  b Describe how the land is divided in map B (i).
  c How is the land divided in map B (ii)?
  d What other differences can you find between the two maps?
  e What took place in Strettington which would account for the differences between the two maps?
  f What features have not changed? Can you suggest why?

13

2.2 Enclosing the commons

C Extract from a petition to the House of Commons, 1797.

" . . . on account of the enclosure of the open fields, commons and waste [of village of Raunds, Northamptonshire] the cottagers . . . entitled to commons rights will be deprived of the privilege of keeping cattle and sheep . . . a more ruinous effect of this enclosure will be the almost total depopulation of their village. . . . They will be driven by want of employment . . . into manufacturing towns where the nature of their employment will soon waste their strength. . . ."

D Extract from 'View of the Agriculture of Middlesex' by John Middleton, published in 1798.

" . . . no sooner does an enclosure take place than the scene is agreeably changed from a dreary waste to the more pleasing one, of the same spot appearing all animation, activity and bustle. Every man capable of performing such operations, is furnished with plenty of employment, in sinking ditches and drains, in making banks and hedges, and in planting quicks [hawthorn bushes] and trees. Nor are the wheelwright, carpenter, smith and other rural artificers [craftsmen] under the necessity of being idle spectators of the scene, since abundance of work will be found for them in the erection of farm-houses . . . and in the forming and making . . . roads, bridges, gates, stiles, implements of husbandry [farming tools], etc. Even . . . when these kind of temporary exertions are over, by the whole being brought into a regular system of husbandry, it will still continue to provide both food and employment for a very increased population."

E Extract from the Board of Agriculture's 'General Report on Enclosures', 1808.

"Wedmore in Somerset
Within twenty years there have been enclosed upwards of 3,000 acres of rich moor land. Before, when it was in commons, it was useless because of flooding six or seven months in the year; when used as pasture for the remaining months, it was of little value, because too many animals were put on it; which land is now let from 30*s* [£1.50p] to 60*s* [£3] per acre. These enclosures are made by ditches, which by annual cleansing and spreading the contents over the surface, afford an excellent manure. This has also created work whereby the poor-rate has been reduced."

3 *Read Source* C .
   a In 1797 a Bill was introduced into the House of Commons to enclose the village of Raunds. Were the petitioners in Source C in favour of enclosure or not?
   b Usually, wealthy landowners petitioned over enclosure. On whose behalf was the petition in Source C presented?
   c What arguments were used by the petitioners to support their case?
   d Is the petition stating facts or expressing opinions? Explain your answer.

4 *Read Source* D .
   a What kinds of employment would be created as a result of enclosing the land?
   b Did the author expect the increase in employment to be of a temporary or permanent nature? Explain why.

5 *Read Source* E .
   a Why did the author claim that the land was 'useless' and 'of little value' before enclosure?
   b What measures had been taken to improve the land?
   c How long had it taken to bring about the improvements?

Linking evidence

6 Which of the Sources favour the enclosure of the commons?

7 Which Sources would support the following:
   (i)   that enclosure led people to leave their villages;
   (ii) that enclosure encouraged improved farming methods and led to increased output from the land;
   (iii) that enclosure led to increased employment?

8 From the evidence in the Sources can you suggest:
   (i) which people might gain by, and therefore favour, enclosure;
   (ii) which people might lose by, and therefore oppose, enclosure.

9 Comparing all the Sources, which in your opinion would be of most use to an historian trying to make an accurate assessment of the results of enclosure? Explain your answer.

10 If you had been a cottager (source A) living in an open field village would you have been in favour of petitioning for enclosure or would you have opposed it? Use evidence from any of the Sources A to E to support your answer.

3.1 The changing fortunes of the handloom weavers

A Scene inside a weaver's cottage.

B Extract from 'The Origin of the New System of Manufacture' by W. Radcliffe, published in 1828.

". . . From 1788 to 1803, I will call the golden age of this great trade. . . . The mule [spinning machine invented by Samuel Crompton] . . . now coming into the vogue [becoming popular] for the warp as well as weft [vertical and horizontal threads in a piece of cloth], added to the water twist [water frame] and common jenny yarns [yarns spun on the 'Spinning Jenny' machine, invented by James Hargreaves], with an increasing demand for every fabric the loom could produce, put all hands in request of every age and description . . . the old loom shops being insufficient, every lumber-room, even old barns, carthouses, and outbuildings of every description, were repaired, windows broke through the old blank walls, and all fitted up for loomshops. . . .

. . . Their dwellings and small gardens clean and neat – all the family well clad – the men with each a watch in his pocket, and the women dressed to their own fancy . . . every house well furnished with a clock . . . handsome tea services . . . and ornaments . . . many cottage families had their cow. . . ."

C Letter from a Bury weaver printed in the 'Manchester Observer', 22 August 1818 and quoted in 'The Condition of the Working Class in 1844' by F. Engels.

"Of all the workers who compete against machinery the most oppressed are the handloom weavers in the cotton industry . . . and even when in full employment cannot earn more than 10s [50p] a week. One branch of hand weaving after another is challenged by the power-loom . . . handloom weaving is the refuge of workers who have lost their livelihood in other sections . . . there is always a surplus of hand-loom weavers . . . they consider themselves fortunate if on the average they can earn between 6s and 7s [between 30p and 35p] a week for fourteen to eighteen hours a day. . . . Frequently half a dozen . . . some of them married . . . live together in a cottage which has one or two workrooms and one large common bedroom. They live almost entirely upon potatoes, supplemented perhaps with a little porridge. They seldom drink milk and they hardly ever eat meat. A large number of them are Irish or of Irish descent. These poor wretches are the first to be thrown out of work when there is a commercial crisis and last to be taken on again when trade improves."

D Graph showing the numbers of handloom weavers and the numbers of power looms in factories between 1820 and 1870.

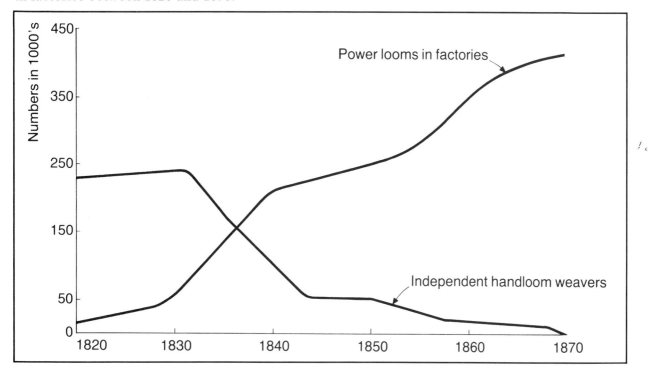

Questions

1 *Look at Source* A .
   a Is the weaving in this picture being done on handlooms or power-looms? How do you know?
   b What other manufacturing process is being carried out?

2 *Read Source* B .
   a What was the 'great trade' referred to in this Source?
   b Why was the period 1788–1803 considered to be a 'golden age' for handloom weavers?
   c What evidence in Source B indicates that an increasing number of handlooms were being set up?
   d Why was it necessary to provide additional windows in 'old blank walls'?
   e What evidence in Source B suggests that the handloom weavers were prosperous?

3 *Read Source* C .
   Was the author of Source C sympathetic or not to the plight of the handloom weavers? Support your answer with evidence from this Source.

4 *Look at Source* D .
   a Approximately how many handloom weavers were there: (i) in 1820; and (ii) in 1830?
   b In which decade did the numbers of handloom weavers fall most rapidly?
   c In approximately which year were there equal numbers of handloom weavers and power looms?
   d In the 1830s a handloom weaver could weave two large pieces of cotton cloth per week; a power-loom weaver could weave nine times as much. How does this information help to explain the changes recorded on the graph?

3.2   The changing fortunes of the handloom weavers

E **Extract from the evidence of W. Hickson on the handloom weavers, taken from 'Parliamentary Papers' of 1840.**
". . . The great majority of hand-loom cotton weavers work in cellars. . . . The reason cellars are chosen is, that cotton requires to be woven damp. . . . I have seen them working in cellars dug out of an undrained swamp . . . the water therefore running down the bare walls. . . .

A great mistake prevails as to the extent to which factory labour . . . is unfavourable to the health and morals of a community, or the happiness of domestic life . . . one . . . confines himself to a single room, in which he eats, drinks and sleeps, and breathes an impure air. The other has not only the exercise of walking to and from the factory, but, when there, lives and breathes in a large roomy apartment in which the air is constantly changed."

F **Power looms.**

5 *Read Source* E .

  a Which two different methods of weaving are compared in this Source?

  b What reason is given for the handloom cotton weavers often working and living in cellars?

  c What were the likely effects of such conditions on the health of the handloom weavers?

  d What important differences do you notice between the descriptions of domestic and factory labour?

  e Does the author of Source E favour the use of the handloom in the home or the power loom in the factory? Quote from this Source to support your answer.

6 *Look at Source* F .

  a How can you tell that this shows a scene inside a factory?

  b What process is being carried out?

  c What do you notice about the people working at the machines?

Linking evidence

7 a   Draw a chart to record the main differences in the conditions of the handloom weavers between the 1790s and 1818. Example:

The Changing Fortunes of the Handloom Weavers	
The Weavers in 1790s	The Weavers in 1818
(complete from Source B)	(complete from Source C)

  b What questions might an historian ask about the differences recorded?

8 Which of the Sources (A – F) attempt to make comparisons between handloom weaving and power-loom weaving?

9 What are the main differences between the two scenes shown in Sources A and F ? Are there any similarities?

10 In which of the two scenes would accidents be most likely to happen? Can you suggest why?

11 Would *you* have preferred to work at the handloom in the weaver's cottage, or the power loom in the factory? Say why.

12 a Give one example of a Source (A – F) which could be described as factual.

  b Give one example of a Source (A – F) in which the author is mainly expressing his opinion.

  c Do you think any of these Sources are biased? If so, explain which ones and why you think this.

13 Given the evidence in Sources A – F , why might the handloom weavers still want to continue working by the method shown in Source A ?

14 Which of the Sources (A – F) suggest that working in a factory may be better than working at home? Which of the Sources (A – F) disagree with this point of view?

15 'Even by 1820, a few power looms had a huge effect on the handloom weavers out of all proportion to their numbers'. Which two Sources could you use to support this point of view? Explain your answer.

4 The Luddites

A Copy of a letter sent to a Huddersfield millowner in 1812 (**Public Record Office, Home Office Papers 40/41**).

"Sir,

Information has just been given in, that you are a holder of those detestable Shearing Frames, and I was desired by many men to . . . give you . . . warning to pull them down . . . if they are not taken down by the end of next week, I shall detach one of my lieutenants with at least 200 men to destroy them . . . burning your buildings down to ashes . . . if you . . . fire at . . . my men, they have orders to murder you and burn all your Housing . . . go to your neighbours to inform them that the same Fate awaits them if their Frames are not taken down . . . we will never lay down our arms till the House of Commons passes an act to put down all the machinery hurtfull . . . to the Commonality . . . but we petition no more, that won't do, fighting must,

Signed by the General of the Army of Redressers,

NED LUDD *Clerk*"

C Extract from Public Record Office, Yorkshire, Document No. TS11/813/2676/21703.

"The disturbances within the West Riding of this County caused by a set of People calling themselves Luddites . . . had risen to so serious . . . a height . . . that . . . the Civic power was no longer . . . effectual to afford protection to Individuals and their property . . . within which . . . Mills . . . a certain kind of Improved Machinery or finishing frames (used in the dressing and finishing of woollen cloth) had been introduced. . . .

Such was the case . . . at . . . William Cartwrights' of Rawfolds . . . Huddersfield . . . a water mill . . . working . . . improved machinery . . . which . . . was publicly known to the Croppers or Shear Men would be defended by W. Cartwright and a Guard of Soldiers . . . it is said . . . 10 important places where this kind of . . . Machinery had been used . . . had been unlawfully . . . destroyed by the Luddites, who . . . concentrated upon a ground attack on W. Cartwright . . . and giving the death blow to the use of this kind of machinery . . . which was known to be defended by a Military Guard. . . ."

B An artist's view of a group of Luddites leading an attack on a mill.

> **D** 'The croppers' song',
> from 'The Rising of the Luddites'
> by Frank Peel (1895 edition).
>
> "Come cropper lads of high renown
> Who love to drink good ale that's brown
> And strike each haughty tyrant down,
> With hatchet, pike and gun!
>
> *Chorus:* Oh, the cropper lads for me,
> Who with lusty stroke
> The shear frames broke
> The cropper lads for me

Questions

1 *Read Source* A .
  a Is this a primary or a secondary source? Explain your answer.
  b The shearmen or croppers carried out some of the finishing stages in the manufacture of woollen cloth. Did they oppose the introduction of steam-driven shearing-gig machinery: (i) because the machines were imported; (ii) because it was difficult to use the new machines; (iii) because it caused unemployment and lower wages? Explain your answer.
  c What threats were made by 'Ned Ludd' to try to get the shearing frames removed?
  d What did the Luddites want Parliament to do?
  e It is doubtful whether such a person as Ned Ludd existed. Does this mean that the Source is unreliable?

2 *Look at Source* B .
  a What weapons are being carried by the Luddites?
  b How does the artist suggest the Luddites met after dark?
  c What appears to be the role of the women shown in the picture? Are they urging the Luddites on, or trying to restrain them? Explain your answer.
  d Does the artist present a sympathetic or unsympathetic view of the Luddites? Explain your answer by referring to features in the picture and the methods used by the artist.

3 *Read Source* C .
  a Why might the owner of Rawfolds Mill not expect to have been attacked by the Luddites?
  b Why did the Luddites concentrate their efforts on Rawfolds Mill?
  c Two Luddites were killed by the military who were defending Rawfolds Mill. What were the likely effects on: (i) the Luddites themselves; (ii) the West Riding millowners?

4 *Read Source* D .
  a How might such a song help bring in new Luddite members?
  b Who do you think were the 'haughty tyrants' referred to in the song?
  c What effect might this song have had on a millowner using the new shearing frames?
  d Does the fact that this Source is a song mean that it is of little use to an historian? Explain.

Linking evidence

5 In 1812 an Act of Parliament made machine-breaking punishable by death. Using evidence from Sources A – D suggest why the Government took the Luddite threat so seriously.

6 This period was one of social and economic distress. Do you consider that machine breaking was justified? Choose one of the following answers and give reasons for your choice.
  (i) Yes, because the Luddites were trying to protect their livelihood.
  (ii) No, because it could not solve the basic problems of the time.
  (iii) It is difficult to decide without more evidence.

5.1 The factory children

A **Extract from 'Letters from England' by R. Southey, published in 1807.**

"Mr – – – remarked that nothing could be so beneficial to a country as manufactures. 'You see these children, sir', said he. 'In most parts of England poor children are a burthen to their parents and to the parish; here the parish, which would else have to support them, is rid of all expense; they get their bread almost as soon as they can run about, and by the time they are seven or eight years old bring in money. There is no idleness among us:- they come at five in the morning, we allow them half an hour for breakfast, and an hour for dinner, they leave work at six, and another set relieves them for the night; the wheels never stand still'. I was looking, while he spoke, at the unnatural dexterity with which the fingers of these little creatures were playing in the machinery, half giddy myself with the noise and the endless motion; and when he told me there was no rest in these walls, day or night, I thought that if Dante [a famous Italian poet who wrote an epic poem, 'The Divine Comedy', one of whose sections describes Hell] had peopled one of his hells with children, here was a scene worthy to have supplied him with new images of torment."

B **A cartoonist's view of factory conditions.**

C Evidence of John Moss, master of the apprentices at a Lancashire mill in 1816 to the Factories Inquiry Commission.

"Q *What were the hours of work?*
A From 5 o'clock in the morning till 8 at night all the year through.
Q *What time was allowed for meals?*
A Half an hour for breakfast and half an hour for dinner.
Q *Would the children sit or stand at work?*
A Stand.
Q *The whole of the time?*
A Yes.
Q *Were they usually much fatigued at night?*
A Yes.
Q *Did you inspect their beds?*
A Yes. There were always some of them missing, some might be run away, others I have found asleep in the mill, on the mill-floor.
Q *Were any children injured by machinery?*
A Very frequently. Very often fingers were crushed, and one had his arm broken.
Q *Were any children deformed?*
A Yes, several. There were two or three that were very crooked."

Questions

1 *Read Source* **A** .
   a What reasons were put forward to justify the employment of young children?
   b Which words or phrases suggest that the visitor, the author of this Source, disapproved of the employment of young children in mills and factories?
   c Both people quoted in this Source observed the same scene. How do you account for them holding such differing views on the employment of children?
   d What information in this Source could be described as 'eye-witness' evidence?
   e What further evidence might an historian wish to consult before assessing the two different views expressed in this Source?

2 *Look at Source* **B** .
   a What is the subject of the cartoon?
   b Was the cartoonist, George Cruikshank, in favour of, or opposed to, the employment of children in textile factories?
   c How does the cartoonist use the written captions to make his point? What other means does he use?

3 *Read Source* **C** .
   a Why might this be a useful Source for an historian studying factory conditions? Give more than one reason.
   b Was the person giving evidence involved in the employment of children? What is his point of view? Quote from the Source to explain your answer.
   c What evidence would support the view that children were overworked and exhausted? Give more than one example.
   d In 1819 a Factory Act was passed to limit the working hours of children, especially pauper apprentices. How might evidence such as that in Source **C** have helped in getting the Bill through Parliament?

5.2 The factory children

D Children working in a cotton spinning factory.

E Evidence of a piecer at a Leicester spinning mill to the Factories Inquiry Commission, 1833.

"I was very nigh nine years of age when I first went to piece [a piecer was someone employed in a spinning factory to join the threads that broke on the machines]. I got 2s 6d [12½p] at first . . . When I had been there half a year I got 3s [15p] . . . I used sometimes to fall asleep. . . . They always strapped us if we fell asleep . . . I ran away because Thorpe used to come and strap me. He did not know what he was strapping me for . . . he would strap anyone as did not please him. . . .

. . . I never told my mother but one time, and that was when there were marks on me. She told me not to mind; she'd give me a halfpenny [less than 1p] to go again and be a good boy. . . . When I ran away, my mother ran after me and would have beat me if she could have catched me. She said she would give me it if I did not get back to the factory. I always paid my wages to my mother."

F Extract from 'Notes of a Tour in the Manufacturing Districts of Lancashire'.

". . . let us grant that juvenile labour is wrong, there is something still worse, and that is juvenile starvation. I have seen with some pain, the little piecers and cleaners employed in their dull work. . . . I thought how much more delightful would have been the gambol of free limbs on the hillside, the inhaling of the fresh breeze. . . . But I have seen other sights. I have seen children perishing from sheer hunger in the mud hovel, or in the ditch by the way-side. I have seen the juvenile beggar and the juvenile tramp with famine in their cheeks and despair in their hearts. . . . I would rather see boys and girls earning their living in the mill, than starving by the roadside . . . or carried in a van to prison. . . ."

4 *Look at Source* D .
  a The child marked at (1) was employed as a 'scavenger' to pick up bits of cotton and to sweep up under the spinning machinery. Describe the position of the child, particularly in relation to the machinery.
  b The spinning machines marked (2) and (3) worked in the same way. The machine marked (2) is fully extended but (3) is not. Note the wheels and runners on the factory floor. From this information and using the illustration can you describe how the machines moved? Why might this be dangerous for children working as 'scavengers'?
  c The 'piecer' marked (4) mended the broken cotton threads. Why could the piecer only work when the machines were fully extended?
  d The machinery was so noisy that workers were unable to hear each other speak. Cotton pieces and dust filled the air. Can you imagine what a working day was like for the child marked at (1)? In no more than 100 words give an account of your first day as a 'scavenger' in a cotton factory (use the information in other Sources if you wish).

5 *Read Source* E .
  a A piecer mended the spun threads which had broken on the machinery. Why do you think spinners often punished their piecers?
  b Can you suggest why the mother wanted her son to continue working in the spinning mill even though he was being beaten?
  c The 1819 Factory Act had tried to limit the working hours of children in some factories. What evidence suggests that the Act was not successful?

6 *Read Source* F .
  a Does the author approve of juvenile (child) labour?
  b What condition does he consider to be even worse for children than employment in a mill?
  c From the evidence, give one *fact* and one *opinion* implied by the author.

Linking evidence

7 Does the evidence in Source E support or oppose the view shown by the cartoonist (Source B)? Explain your answer.

8 Which of the Sources (A – F) contain evidence which might be used to support the case for the employment of children in the mills? Give two examples.

9 Using Sources A – F to help you, what other questions would you have asked John Moss in Source C about conditions in the textile mill at that time? What answers do you think he might have given?

10 Source E gives the boy's view of events. Does the fact that his mother tried to force him to go back to the mill mean that she was a cruel person? In a short paragraph, try to express the views she might have given at the time. Use other Sources in this topic to help you.

11 Using the written and pictorial evidence, write a letter to an MP urging him to support a Factory Bill limiting the working hours of children, improving conditions and appointing factory inspectors.

6 The North-East Coalfield

A **Plan of the River Tyne and surrounding area, 1804 (section).**

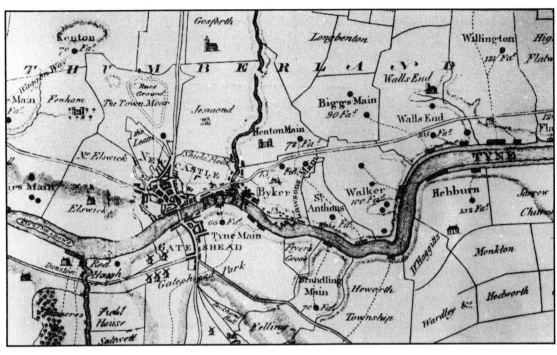

B **Extract from a traveller's description of Newcastle, 1784.**

"The coal-mines in the neighbourhood of Newcastle are . . . numerous. . . . Vessels loaded with coal, for London and different parts of Europe, sail daily from this port . . . every hour of the day. . . . The winding machine which raises the coal from the pit is . . . easily worked by two stout horses. . . . Waggons . . . carry it to wharfs on the river side. . . .

Roads . . . are formed . . . to the place where the vessels are loaded.

. . . four-wheeled waggons . . . move along the inclined plane . . . until they reach the Tyne. Arrived there, a . . . wooden frame prolongs the road . . . at such a height above the water as to permit vessels to pass below it. . . . A man stationed on the platform opens a hatch. . . . When the waggon comes to the trap in the platform it stops . . . and all the coal runs . . . through the hopper into the vessel. . . ."

KEY

- ● Coal-mine/pit. Depths of pits shown in fathoms.
- — River staithes or wharves.
- --- Waggonways.

(Scale 1 inch to 1 mile)

C **Extract from the evidence of J. Buddle on the state of the coal trade in 1829, given before the Select Committee of the House of Lords.**

"Q *Have you any calculations of the number of men and ships employed on the two rivers [Rivers Tyne and Wear]?*

A I have made a summary: there are, seamen 15,000, pitmen and above ground people employed at the collieries 21,000, keelmen, coal boatmen, casters and trimmers, 2,000, making the total number employed in what I call the Northern coal trade 38,000. . . ."

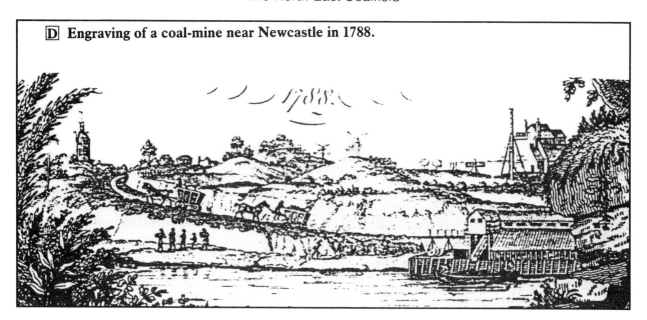

D Engraving of a coal-mine near Newcastle in 1788.

Questions

1 *Look at Source* **A** .
  a How many coal wharves or staithes (marked ▬) can you find along the banks of the River Tyne? What have all of them in common?
  b Which was the most important coal port? Explain your answer.
  c Can you suggest any difficulties in using the River Tyne for river navigation?

2 *Read Source* **B** .
  a What evidence indicates that the North-East had a thriving coasting and export trade in coal?
  b What form of power was used to raise coal from the pits and to carry it to the wharves?
  c Is this a primary or a secondary Source? Explain your answer.

3 *Read Source* **C** .
  a What was the Select Committee of the House of Lords inquiring into?
  b John Buddle was a leading mining engineer. Does the fact that he was giving evidence mean that this Source is completely reliable? Explain your answer.
  c What do you notice about all the figures provided by Buddle? Why might this make you suspect that they might not all be accurate?
  d What questions should an historian ask before making use of this Source?

4 *Look at Source* **D** .
Describe in your own words the scene shown, mentioning the following: the use of steam power, the waggonway, the shutes at the loading wharves and the flat barges.

Linking evidence

5 List all the features described in Source **B** which can be identified in Source **D** .

6 Why might an historian find it useful to have a written source (**B**) and a picture source (**D**) from approximately the same period of time and from the same geographical area?

7 What other evidence can you find in Sources **A** , **B** and **D** to support Buddle's view of the importance of the coal trade in this area?

27

7 The miners' safety lamp

A **Extract from 'British Social and Economic History from 1760 to the Present Day' by P. Lane, published in 1979.**

"As mines became deeper there was . . . increasing danger from the gas 'fire-damp'. When this gas came into contact with the naked light of the candle stuck into the miner's hat, it exploded. Unfortunately, candles were the only form of underground lighting they knew. In 1812 a . . . serious mine disaster in Sunderland roused public interest. Sir Humphry Davy [was] a famous scientist, . . . already well-known for his work on chlorine, electricity and laughing-gas. The mine disaster led Davy to invent a new miners' lamp. Men could now work in the deeper gas-ridden mines with some degree of safety."

B **A letter from Sir Humphry Davy.**

> "Octr 30 1815
> 23 Grosvenor Street

Dear Sir

I shall inclose, with this a notice of my results on the fire damp – My experiments have been successful far-beyond my hopes – I hope in a very short time to be able to send models of the different lamps for Mr Buddle & Mr Dunn & for the collieries in your neighbourhood.

> I am Dear Sir
> very sincerely yours
> H. Davy"

C **Extract from the evidence of John Moody, quoted in 'Longman Secondary History Packs'.**

". . . On . . . 21 October 1815, at 6 o'clock in the evening, I accompany'd Mr Stephenson and Mr Wood down a pit at Killingworth Colliery in purpose to try Mr Stephenson's first safety lamp at a Blower. But when we came near the Blower it was making so much more gas than usual that I told Mr Stephenson and Mr Wood if the lamp should deceive him we should be severely burnt, but Mr Stephenson would insist upon the tryal. . . . So Mr Wood and I went . . . at a distance and left Mr Stephenson to himself. . . ."

Evidence of George Stephenson on the same occasion.

"When I approached towards the blower . . . I carried my lamp very slow and steady to observe the alteration of the flame in the lamp. . . . I observed the flame increasing in size and change its colour to a kind of blue. I went a little further, the flame then went out. I then told my companions the effect and in a short time my companions became more bold so that they went up with me and see'd the gas burn within the lamp."

D **Quote attributed to Sir Humphry Davy, used in 'The First Industrial Revolution' ('Longman Secondary History Packs').**

"I never heard a word of George Stephenson and his lamp until six weeks after my principle of security had been published and the general impression of the scientific men in London is that Stephenson had some loose idea floating in his mind which he had unsuccessfully attempted to put into practice till after my labours were made known."

E **Extract from the 'First Report of Mines Inspectors' in 1851.**

"Six persons have been burnt to death by firedamp when using the Davy lamp. . . .

Davy . . . warned the miner not to expose it [the lamp] to a rapid current of inflammable air unless protected by a shield half encircling the gauze.

. . . the gauze [of the lamp] is seen at times red hot, and smeared outside with grease and coal dust, whereby the risk of ignition is rendered more imminent. . . .

. . . The Davy lamp . . . is disliked by the miner on account of the feeble illumination and he is sometimes tempted to take off the gauze. . . ."

Questions

1 *Read Source* A .
   a This is a secondary source. How can you tell?
   b Do you think the disaster described was the *only* reason for the invention of the lamp? Choose one of the following answers and give reasons for your choice. (i) Yes, because it is stated in a history textbook. (ii) No, because changes in history are usually the result of a number of factors. (iii) There is insufficient evidence to make a judgement.

2 *Read Source* B .
   a In 1815, the Society for the Prevention of Mining Accidents was set up in Sunderland. Can you suggest the connection between fire damp, the Sunderland Society, and the experiments of Davy into 'different lamps'?
   b Why was Davy sending 'models' to John Buddle of Wallsend, a leading mining engineer who was interested in improving underground ventilation?
   c In what way was the author of Source B involved in the situation he describes? Why does this make it an important Source for an historian?

3 *Read Source* C .
   a What was the purpose of the visit to Killingworth Colliery on 21 October 1815?
   b A 'blower' is a crack from which gas escapes. Why did Stephenson approach it with his lamp?
   c Why was Moody nervous about conducting the experiment on this occasion?
   d If you had been in Killingworth Colliery at that time would you have stood with Moody and Wood, or would you have accompanied George Stephenson? Say why.
   e How successful was the experiment? Explain your answer.
   f Give one example of a *fact*, and one example of an *opinion* from Source C .

4 *Read Source* D .
   a What is Davy suggesting about Stephenson's development of a safety lamp?
   b How might an historian attempt to check the accuracy of Davy's suggestions as to the timing of the invention of the first successful miners' lamp?
   c Davy was a famous scientist working in London; Stephenson was an engineer working in the North-East. Which man had the greater opportunities to inform the public of his work?

5 *Read Source* E .
   a Do you think this Source is likely to be a reliable piece of evidence? Explain why.
   b The Davy lamp was intended to increase safety in the mines by preventing explosions from 'fire damp'. (i) Why did serious accidents still occur? (ii) Why did some coalminers ignore safety warnings when using the lamp?

Linking evidence

6 From the evidence in Sources A – E give one example of a *cause* and one example of a *result* of the invention of the miners' safety lamp.

7 Historians often have to compare Sources which provide conflicting evidence. In what ways is the evidence in Source E (primary source) in conflict with Source A (secondary source)?

8 Sources A – E provide evidence of the *short-term* and the *long-term* results of the use of the safety lamp. Give one example of each.

8 The Rotherham Ironworks

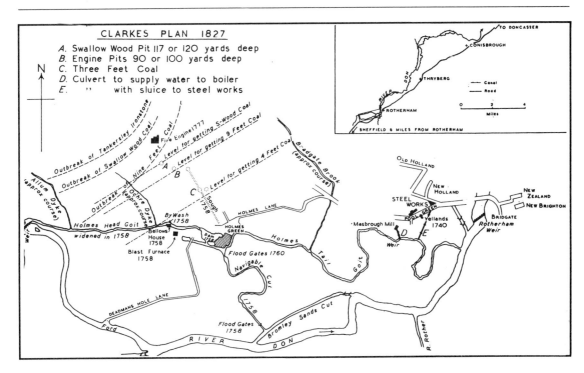

CLARKES PLAN 1827

A. Swallow Wood Pit 117 or 120 yards deep
B. Engine Pits 90 or 100 yards deep
C. Three Feet Coal
D. Culvert to supply water to boiler
E.   ,,   with sluice to steel works

A Map of the Rotherham Ironworks
and the surrounding area.

B Extract describing Samuel Walker's ironworks in 1781, taken from the 'Memorandum Book' of Samuel Walker.
"At Holme . . . pulled down two shops to make room for the new Fire Engine [steam engine] and rebuilt 'em in the same yard with improvements . . . turned the brewhouse at the Hall into a dwelling house . . . built and covered in a new Fire Engine house (this a very heavy job) . . . about Holme . . . an additional warehouse . . . pulled down two small pot furnaces and built a larger in lieu of [instead of] both also a new warehouse at the bottom of the yard . . . Jordan Dam . . . New pitched above 20 yards [18 metres] long of the Wash with Ashlar brest wall . . . with a large job of Ashlar work adjoining above and below . . . very heavy jobs. . . . Sam. Walker built another wing to his house being a large addition to his ale cellar with a room over it. . . ."

C Extract from a letter from Samuel Walker to Messrs. Boulton and Watt, ordering a Boulton and Watt steam engine.
"Rotherham, May 15th, 1781
. . . We have some Works upon a river . . . but in dry Seasons we are much retarded for want of Water . . . to make up this defect . . . we are intending to build a Fire Engine [steam engine], either in the old . . . manner, or under the Sanction of your Patent . . . We have Coal of our own getting laid down at the Work at about 2¾d [2p] (per) cwt and . . . suppose we may work the Engine 3 to 6 Months in the Year, according as the Seasons are wet or dry – Query, on what Terms we can be permitted to go on with. . . .
We hope you will be moderate in your demands, which may be a means of introducing your Engines into this County. . . . Your reply *as soon as you can* will oblige. . . ."

Questions

1 *Look at Source* A .
  a What is this Source and what does it show?
  b In what way might this type of Source be useful to an historian?
  c There were supplies of local charcoal in the area. Which other raw materials and fuel were available for the Rotherham iron and steel works?
  d From the position of the Bellows House can you suggest which form of power was used to enable hot air to be blown into the Blast Furnace?
  e In which year was a navigable cut constructed? How did it help in the supply of raw materials and in the export of finished goods?
  f What was constructed in 1758 and 1760 to prevent the navigable cut from flooding?
  g What was constructed in 1758 to help increase the supply of water?
  h How was water drained from the coal-pits?
  i Which year was marked by the greatest progress for the Rotherham Ironworks? Why should an ironworks have prospered in the period of the Seven Years War (1756–63)?
  j A fire engine (steam engine) is shown to have been set up in 1777. From its position on the map, can you suggest what it was used for?

2 *Read Source* B .
  a Was the Rotherham Ironworks located at Holmes Green expanding or contracting in 1781? Provide evidence from the Source to support your answer.
  b What evidence indicates that Samuel Walker was prospering?

3 *Read Source* C .
  a For what purpose did Samuel Walker intend to install a fire engine (steam engine) in 1781?
  b What are 'the works upon a River' referred to in this Source?
  c The request to Boulton and Watt was written in May. What phrase in the extract indicates that the problem faced by the ironworks was urgent at that time of the year?
  d Which phrase in the extract indicates that Samuel Walker wanted to get the fire engine (steam engine) as cheaply as possible? How did he suggest that Boulton and Watt might benefit if a steam engine of the new design was built at Rotherham?

Linking evidence

4 What evidence in Source B suggests that Boulton and Watt reached an agreement with Samuel Walker regarding the steam engine discussed in Source C ?

5 From the evidence in Sources A – C can you suggest some of the advantages in siting an ironworks in the Rotherham area?

6 Until around 1760 the British iron industry had been held back by three problems: shortage of fuel, shortage of power and shortage of transport. Explain how the location of the Rotherham Ironworks and the improvements made by Samuel Walker provided solutions to these problems.

9 The steam engine

A Extract from the official document granting a patent to James Watt.
"1769 Patent . . . I James Watt of Glasgow in Scotland Merchant . . . Whereas . . . King George the Third by his Letters Patent . . . did Give and Grant unto me . . . his special Licence full power Sole privilege that I . . . might . . . use . . . and sell . . . my New Invented Method of Lessening the Consumption of Steam and fuel in fire Engines [i.e. *steam engines*]. . . ."

B Letter to James Watt from Matthew Boulton of the Soho Ironworks near Birmingham.
"7 February 1769. I was excited by two motives to offer you my assistance which were love of you and love of a money-getting ingenious project. I presumed that your engine would require money, very accurate workmanship and . . . my idea was to settle a manufactory near to my own where I would erect all the conveniences for the completion of engines, and from which manufactory we would serve all the world with engines of all sizes . . . we could engage and instruct some excellent workmen . . . execute the invention . . . cheaper than it would be otherwise executed, and with as great a difference of accuracy as there is between the blacksmith and the mathematical instrument maker. It would not be worth my while to make for three counties only, but I find it very well worth my while to make for all the world."

C Extracts from evidence given to a Parliamentary Committee, recorded in the 'House of Commons Journal', 1775.
"*John Roebuck, M.D.* . . . that £2000 at the least had been expended in bringing the Fire Engines [steam engine] to their present state . . . this engine . . . will at least do double the work of a common fire engine at the same expense . . . it may be applied wherever any kind of mechanical power is wanted. . . . He is of opinion the money already expended, together with a moderate stock to carry this invention into execution may amount to £10,000 . . . boring and turning mills for making of cylinders; and foundries for casting them . . . will cost a very considerable sum of money. . . .
Matthew Boulton, Esquire . . . A very large sum of money will be required to carry this invention into execution. . . . It is not only the cheapest mechanical power yet invented except wind and water mills, but it may be applied to . . . purposes to which the common fire engine is not at all applicable. . . . He had great reason to believe that if this invention was once established into a regular manufactory, great numbers of engines would be exported to . . . the European continent. . . ."

D Extract from a letter from Matthew Boulton to the Earl of Dartmouth.
"1775, February 22.
. . . the great utility of steam or fire engines in collieries, in lead, tin, and copper mines, and in other great works where great power is required . . . Mr Watt's intentions, if carried into execution, will very much extend the utility of fire engines by rendering them one-fourth of the expenses usual, and by adapting them to a great variety of purposes and manufactures to which the present engines cannot be applied. . . . In . . . 1769, he took out a patent. . . . But as a great part of the time of his patent is elapsed . . . and as a large sum of money must yet be expended before any advantage can be gained from it, I think that his abilities and my money may be otherwise better employed, unless parliament be pleased to grant a prolongation of the term of his exclusive privilege. . . ."

Questions

1 *Read Source* A .
   a What powers did the 'letters patent' grant to James Watt?
   b The Newcomen engine had been used since the early eighteenth century but was expensive in fuel (coal) consumption. In what ways was Watt's engine an improvement?

2 *Read Source* B .
   a Matthew Boulton gives two reasons for assisting James Watt. What were they, and which do you think was uppermost in his mind?
   b What would James Watt and Matthew Boulton each gain from a business association? Give more than one example.
   c James Watt was a mathematical/scientific instrument maker. How does Boulton use this information to flatter him?
   d In 1769 Watt was in partnership with John Roebuck of the Carron Ironworks in Scotland. Roebuck was only willing to let Boulton make Watt steam engines for local use. Can you explain why it would not be worthwhile for Boulton to 'make for three counties only'?
   e In 1769 Boulton told Watt that there was 'some obstruction to our partnership in the engine trade'. In what ways was Watt's partnership with Roebuck likely to be an 'obstruction'?

3 *Read Source* C .
   a What evidence in Source C indicates that large financial investments were required to develop James Watt's steam engine?
   b How does Source C provide evidence to show that both Roebuck and Boulton believed that the steam engine would be economical to use in comparison with other forms of power?
   c Roebuck owed Boulton money and the latter agreed to take over Roebuck's share of the Watt steam engine in part payment. From the evidence in Source C can you suggest any reason why Roebuck had fallen into debt?

4 *Read Source* D .
   a Is this letter concerned with: (i) granting a new patent; (ii) cancelling a patent; or (iii) the extension of a patent? Explain your answer.
   b Where and for what purposes were early steam engines used?
   c Watt had been granted a patent in 1769. Why did he need to extend it in 1775?
   d Why would Boulton be unwilling to invest his money in developing Watt's steam engine without the extension of the patent?

Linking evidence

5 Which of the Sources A – D provide evidence:
   (i)   of the export potential of James Watt's steam engine;
   (ii) to indicate that the steam engine would provide a cheaper form of energy;
   (iii) of the importance of partnerships in the development of new ideas and inventions?

6 Which of the following factors contributed most to the development of the Watt steam engine: (i) partnerships; (ii) financial investment; (iii) technical skill; (iv) inspiration; (v) the demand for a cheap form of energy? List the factors in order of importance, beginning with the most important.

7 In what ways do Sources A – D provide evidence of the problems and difficulties to be overcome in developing an invention for practical use?

10.1 A Trans-Pennine canal

A **Extract from an article in the 'York Courant', 15 July 1766.**

"Meeting at the Sun Inn

At a Meeting held this 2nd Day of July 1766 . . . in Bradford . . . to consider . . . a Navigation [canal] that will connect the East and West Seas, and communicate with the great Ports and trading Towns of Hull, Leeds, Wakefield, Bradford, Keighley, Skipton, Coln, Burnley, Clithero, Blackburn, Wigan, Liverpool, Preston, and Lancaster, upon consideration of several Plans . . . laid before us, it is the Opinion of this Meeting, that such a Navigation is practicable, and will be of great Utility [use] to the Trade of the Kingdom . . . and particularly to the Counties of York and Lancaster: It is, therefore, resolved that a Subscription be set on Foot for raising Money for effecting [building] the said Navigation. . . ."

B **Extract from the 'House of Commons Journals', 27 February 1770.**

". . . a Survey and Plan of the intended Navigation were produced . . . *John Longbotham* . . . had surveyed the Grounds over which the Navigation was . . . to be carried, and made that Plan . . . he thinks . . . it will be of great Utility to the Country, as there are Coals in some Parts, which are much wanted in others . . . it will open a safe, easy . . . Communication between several trading Towns . . . That the Price of Carriage, by the Canal, would be about Two Pence a Ton per Mile [1p a tonne per 1.6 km], which . . . will be much cheaper than Land Carriage. . . .

Henry Acroyd . . . the Distance from Leeds to Liverpool, by Land, is about 82 measured Miles [131 km], and the Price of Carriage about One Shilling a Mile for a Ton [5p a tonne per 1.6 km]: that, by the Canal, it will be 108½ Miles [173 km], and the Price of Carriage Two Pence a Mile [1p a tonne per 1.6 km]. . . .

James Brindley . . . delivered . . . an Estimate of the Expence of making the proposed Navigation, including the Purchase of Lands, amounting to £269,502 . . . since . . . making . . . that Estimate, he had gone over Part of the Ground again, and found some Reasons for altering this Estimate to £300,000 . . . which . . . includes every possible Expence . . .

ORDERED, That Leave be given to bring in a Bill for making a navigable Cut, or Canal, from Leeds . . . to . . . Liverpool. . . ."

C **Extract from an article in the 'Leeds Intelligencer', 22 March 1774.**

"We hear . . . that 20 miles [32 km] of the Grand Canal between Liverpool and Leeds was opened yesterday for business, from Skipton to below the junction with the Bradford Canal, in the presence of several thousand spectators. From Bingley to about three miles [5 km] downwards. . . . A fivefold, a threefold, a twofold, and a single lock, making together a fall of 120 feet [37 metres]; a large aqueduct bridge of seven arches over the River Aire, and an aqueduct and a large banking over the Shipley Valley. Five boats . . . passed the grand lock, the first of which descended through a fall of sixty feet [18 metres] in less than twenty-nine minutes, to the amazement . . . of the spectators. . . .

This joyful . . . event was welcomed with the ringing of Bingley Bells, a band of music, the firing of guns by the neighbouring Militia, the shouts of the spectators . . . as this is deemed [thought], in many respects, the most difficult part of the work, it gives a pleasing prospect . . . of the whole of this grand . . . undertaking being completed in a few years. . . ."

D The seal of the Leeds
and Liverpool Canal Company.

Questions

1 *Read Source* **A** .
 a According to Source **A** , what was considered at the meeting held at the Sun Inn, Bradford in July 1766?
 b What did those present at the meeting resolve to do?
 c For what purposes were subscriptions raised?
 d Distinguish between *fact* and *opinion* by giving one example of each from this Source.
 e Why might those present at the Sun Inn have wanted the meeting reported in the newspapers?

2 *Read Source* **B** .
 a What is Source **B** ?
 b Why might an historian consider this Source to be a reliable piece of evidence?
 c Source **B** has been edited (cut) for purposes of length. Does this make it a less reliable source? Where could you look to check on this point?
 d The promoters named in Source **B** expected carriage by canal to be much cheaper than by road. Using the estimates given, calculate how much it would cost to carry one ton of goods between Leeds and Liverpool: (i) by land; (ii) by canal. What was the saving estimated to be?
 e How does Source **B** show that the MPs on the House of Commons committee were satisfied with the evidence of the canal promoters?

3 *Read Source* **C** .
 a What evidence indicates that the Leeds and Liverpool Canal was opened in sections?
 b What canal works near Bingley enabled the boats to 'climb' and 'descend' gradients?
 c What is an aqueduct and why were two built on this section of the canal?
 d Why was this section of the canal thought the 'most difficult part of the work'?

4 *Look at Source* **D** .
 a Which two towns are represented by the Liver bird (a) and the sheep fleece (b)?
 b The two roses (c) above the shield would be coloured red and white. Which two counties did they represent?
 c Where would you expect the seal to be used?

10.2   A Trans-Pennine canal

E An account of the incomes and outgoings of the Leeds and Liverpool Canal, 1 January 1788 to 1 January 1789, taken from the 'Memorandum Book' of Joseph Priestley of Bradford.

INCOME

Commodities	Yorkshire Side of Canal				Lancashire Side of Canal			
	Tons	Income			Tons	Income		
		£	s	d		£	s	d
Merchandize	16620½	1710	16	8	7995	1096	9	5
Coals	23961	1107	1	2¾	109209	5330	16	3
Limestone	24972	722	17	11½	1429	18	7	9
Lime and Manure	1776	34	19	8	12224½	181	7	6
Stone, Brick &c.	12607	248	4	9¼	3613	66	15	3¼

OUTGOINGS

Item	Yorkshire Side of Canal			Lancashire Side of Canal		
	£	s	d	£	s	d
Repairs	527	4	6½	1234	14	9½
Damages, Taxes etc.	113	8	3	76	8	4½
Wages and Expences	271	14	10½	161	5	1

	£	s	d
Committees, Salaries and expences chargeable to the concern (as a whole)	417	3	6
Interest of Money	56	2	1

F Plan of the route of the Leeds and Liverpool Canal.

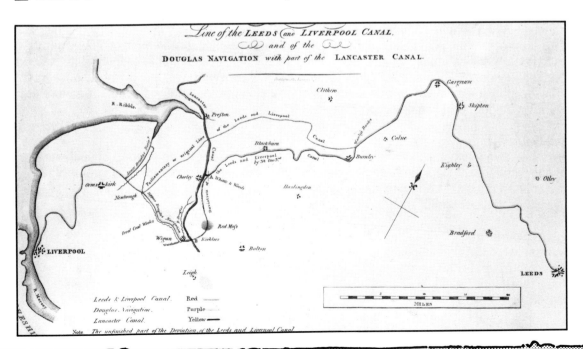

G **Extract from an article in the 'York Chronicle', 31 October 1816.**

"The Canal, from Blackburn to Wigan, was opened on Tuesday . . . 22nd October. The rest of the Canal has been opened at different periods; therefore it is now navigable from Leeds to Liverpool. The barges . . . reached Skipton on Saturday evening . . . the following morning reached Foulridge, where . . . entering the great tunnel the band played a solemn hymn . . . proceeded . . . to Burnley . . . Monday morning . . . on their approach to Blackburn . . . people . . . cheered them . . . reached Wigan in the evening . . . next morning arrived at Liverpool . . . The demonstrations of joy were great."

5 *Look at Source* E *.*
   a What type of evidence is provided here?
   b What was the total tonnage for: (i) the Yorkshire side; and (ii) the Lancashire side of the canal?
   c Which side of the canal: (i) earned the highest income; (ii) cost most in repairs; (iii) had the greatest trade in coal?
   d In a maximum of 100 words describe the similarities and differences in trade between the Yorkshire side and the Lancashire side of the Leeds and Liverpool canal.
   e How might the goods carried on the Leeds and Liverpool canal contribute to the improvement of farming?
   f How might the carriage of building materials lead to changes in the appearance of the towns and villages on or near the canal route?

6 *Look at Source* F *.*
   a Using the scale on the plan, calculate the length of the 'Parliamentary or original Line' of the Leeds and Liverpool Canal.
   b The plan indicates a change or 'deviation' from the original Line. Using the scale on the plan, what mileage was saved as a result of the deviation?
   c Name two towns which were linked to the Leeds and Liverpool canal by branches or shorter canals.
   d In what ways might this evidence be helpful to an historian working on the history of the canal?

7 *Read Source* G *.*
   a When was the last section of the Leeds and Liverpool canal opened?
   b The original Act for the Leeds and Liverpool Canal was passed in 1770. How long did it take to complete the whole navigable waterway?

Linking evidence

8 Compare the estimated costs in Source B with the income and expenditure figures in Source E . Did the canal justify the hopes of the promoters?

9 Use all the evidence provided to write an account of the development of the canal.

NIGHT MAIL.

GENERAL POST-OFFICE.

The EARL OF LICHFIELD, Her Majesty's Postmaster-General.

London to *Preston Rail Way* TIME BILL.

Despatched from the General Post-Office, the   of   183 , at   { With a Time-Piece safe   No.   to

Arrived at the *Rail Way Station*, at   Off at

Names or Numbers of Engines

London and Birmingham Company.

Arrived at *Watford*, at
Arrived at *Tring*, at
Arrived at *Leighton Buzzard*, at
Arrived at *Woberton*, at
Arrived at *Blisworth*, at
Arrived at *Weedon*, at
Arrived at *Rugby*, at
Arrived at *Coventry*, at
Arrived at the *Rail Way Station, Birmingham*, at

Grand Junction Company.

Bescot Bridge
Arrived at *Wolverhampton*, at
Penkridge
Arrived at *Stafford*, at
Norton Bridge
Arrived at *Whitmore*, at
Arrived at *Crewe*, at

North Union Company.

Winsford
Arrived at *Hartford*, at
Preston Brook
Arrived at *Warrington*, at
Newton
Arrived at the *Rail Way Station, Park Side*, at   Off at
Wigan
Chorley Station
Arrived at *Preston Railway Station*, at

Arrived at the Post-Office, Preston, the   of   183 , at   { Delivered the Time-Piece safe   No.   to

By Command of the Postmaster-General,
GEORGE STOW,
Surveyor and Superintendent.

200.—Sept. 1838.

General Post-Office.

The Earl of CHESTERFIELD, } Postmaster-
AND
The Earl of LEICESTER, } General.

London to Exeter Time-Bill.

Dispatched from the General Post-Office, the   of   179 , { With a Time-Piece safe   N°   to

Coach N°   sent out

Arrived at the Gloucester Coffee-house, Piccadilly, at

	Miles	Time allowed H. M.	
Wilson	3¾	3 55	Arrived at Bagshot at 11 . 55
Demezy	20	2 30	Arrived at Hartford Bridge at 2 . 25
W. Wilton	8½	1 10	Arrived at Overton at 3 . 35
Weeks	28½	3 40	Arrived at Salisbury at 7 . 15
		30	To be at Salisbury by a Quarter past Seven, where Thirty Minutes are allowed for Breakfast
Shergold	10	1 20	Arrived at Woodyeats at 9 . 5
Wood	12½	1 40	Arrived at Blandford at 10 . 45
Bryer	16	2 10	Arrived at Dorchester at 12 . 55
		30	Thirty Minutes allowed for Dinner, &c.
Warre	27½	4 0	Arrived at Axminster at 5 . 25
Pine	6½	1 15	Arrived at Honiton at 6 . 40
Land	16	2 10	Arrived at the Post-Office, Exeter, the of 179
179	24	50	at 8 . 50

The Mail to be delivered at the Post-Office, Exeter, Fifty Minutes past Eight in the Evening

Coach N°   arrived   { Delivered the Time-Piece safe   N°   to

By Command of the Postmaster-General,
T. HASKER.

The Time of working each Stage is to be reckoned from the Coach's Arrival. First Minutes for every five Herein, is as much as is necessary, and as the Time whether more or less, is to be sketched up in the Course of the Stage, it is the Coachmen's Duty to be as expeditious as possible, as to report the Horse-keepers if they are not always ready when the Coach arrives, and allow in getting it off.

11 Speeding the mail

Questions

1 *Look at Source* A .

  a What was a 'time-bill' and what information did it provide?

  b What was a 'time piece' and what do you think it was used for?

  c At what time in the morning did the mail coach arrive at Salisbury? How long did it stop there and why?

  d The distance on the London to Exeter route was 179 miles (288 km). What was the average speed for the whole journey (including stops) in miles or kilometres per hour?

  e The names on the left are the contractors along the route who supplied the horses at each stage. How many stages were there between London and Exeter? Which was the longest stage and which was the shortest stage?

  f How many horses pulled each mail coach and how much time was allowed for the changeover at each stage? Can you suggest why the horses had to be changed so many times over a long journey?

2 *Look at Source* B .

  a The London to Preston route involved the use of the engines and carriages of three different railway companies. Can you name them?

  b The distance covered between London and Preston was approximately 221 miles (356 km). What was the average speed for the whole journey (including stops) in miles or kilometres per hour?

Linking evidence

3 In what ways are the *content* and *form* of Source B similar to those of Source A ? Give examples.

4 In what ways is the *content* of Source B different from the *content* of Source A ? Give as many examples as you can.

5 How can you explain the differences in the *content* of the two Sources?

6 What period of time separates the two Sources?

7 What was the difference in the rate of travel (miles/kilometres per hour) between the 'expected' journey time on the London to Exeter route in 1797 and the London to Preston route in 1838?

8 Does the evidence *prove* that important changes had taken place in the methods of transport? Discuss in a short paragraph.

9 Why might the time-bill for the railway journey be more likely to be kept to than the time-bill for the mail coach journey? Explain your answer.

12.1 The Stockton and Darlington Railway

A **Extract from the Cully Manuscripts, Northumberland County Record Office.**

"5 February 1819

A set of merchants and speculators are endeavouring to obtain an Act of Parliament to enable them to make a railway from Stockton to Darlington. . . . The measure is not for the general benefit, and will prove disastrous to those concerned. The . . . projected railway will . . . injure the highly cultivated region . . . and cut and intersect the enclosures which are now laid out at much expense for the purpose of agriculture . . . beside the Darlington line, which passes nearly two miles through my property, a branch is intended to go to Piercebridge through the best part of my property . . . it does not meet with the concurrence of the landed proprietors over whose property it is proposed to carry it, on the contrary it is almost universally opposed by them. . . .

Matthew Cully

To Mr Foster
Queen's Head
Newcastle on Tyne"

B **Extract from 'The Diaries of Edward Pease', edited by Sir A. E. Pease.**

"It was in discussion with Edward Pease that the questions were decided . . . of the composition of rails, when of iron, whether they should be wrought or cast, and of what weight, and what the gauge [width between the rails] of the railway should be. Originally a wooden tramway had been Edward Pease's idea and then iron. Malleable rails in those days of comparatively cheap labour cost £12 a ton, and cast iron ones £5 10s [£5.50p]. These first rails were 'fish bellied', weighing only 28 pounds [12 kilos] to the yard [metre]. . . . The gauge was taken from the road wagons, 4ft 8½ins [1.5 metres]. . . ."

C **Extract from 'The Diaries of Edward Pease', edited by Sir A. E. Pease.**

"Killingworth Colliery
April 28th 1821

Sir,
. . . I am glad to learn that the Bill has passed for the Darlington Railway. . . .

I am willing to undertake to survey and mark out the best line of way within the limits prescribed by the Act of Parliament, and also to assist the Committee with plans and estimates, and in letting to the different contractors such work as they might judge it advisable to do by contract, and . . . to superintend the execution of the work – And I . . . recommend the whole being done by contract. . . .

Were I to contract for the whole line . . . it would be necessary for me to do so at an advanced price upon the sub-contractors, and it would also be necessary for the Committee to have some person to superintend my undertaking. This would be . . . an extra expense and the Committee would derive no advantage to compensate for it. . . .

I remain yours respectfully,
George Stephenson
To Edward Pease Esq."

D **Route of Stockton and Darlington Railway.**

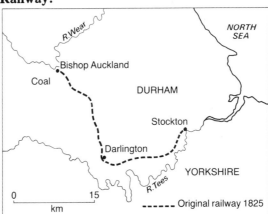

Questions

1 *Read Source* [A] .

  a Who wrote the letter and what was it about?

  b Was the writer of Source [A] a supporter or opponent of the proposed Stockton and Darlington railway?

  c How does Matthew Cully describe the promoters and how does this help to reveal his attitude towards them?

  d He gives a number of reasons for opposing the proposed railway. What do you think was his main objection to it?

  e What evidence suggests that Cully was a large landowner?

  f How had the land through which the railway was to pass been improved for farming?

  g Is Source [A] concerned *mainly* with *fact* or with *opinion*?

  h Source [A] is clearly biased against the proposed railway. Does this mean that it is of no use to an historian? Explain your answer.

  i What further information (other Sources) might be useful to provide a balanced view of the Stockton and Darlington railway project?

2 *Read Source* [B] .

  a The colliery owners around Darlington, and coal traders such as the Quaker businessman and merchant Edward Pease, wanted a cheaper and quicker means of sending coal to Stockton for shipment. In what ways was Pease involved in the technical questions relating to the railway?

  b In what way was the original plan for the railway changed?

  c Can you explain why cast iron and malleable (wrought) iron rails differed so greatly in cost?

  d Can you suggest why wrought iron rails are superior to cast iron rails?

  e What was the final gauge chosen and how was the decision made?

  f Do you consider that this was a sensible way to make the decision about the gauge?

  g How might an historian check the facts and figures given in Source [B] ?

3 *Read Source* [C] .

  a Which two phrases in the letter indicate that the Stockton and Darlington Railway Company had obtained an Act for building the line?

  b Source [C] is a letter of reply from George Stephenson to Edward Pease. What do you think Edward Pease's letter had requested?

  c In what ways was Stephenson willing to help the committee which had been set up to manage the day-to-day affairs of the Company?

  d Is there any evidence which might suggest that Stephenson was a fair and honest man who was not prepared to build railways just for money? Explain your answer.

  e What was needed before a railway or canal could be built? (Refer to Sources [A] and [C] .)

4 *Look at Source* [D] .

  a Using the scale on the map, estimate the length of the railway (in kilometres).

  b Why do you think the railway terminated at Stockton: (i) because it was an important town; (ii) because it was on the border between Yorkshire and Durham; (iii) because it was a port?

  c Why do you think that the railway went as far as Bishop Auckland?

  d Name one of the raw materials that was carried on the railway.

12.2   The Stockton and Darlington Railway

E   Train of waggons crossing the turnpike road near Darlington.

F   The opening of the Stockton to Darlington Railway, 27 September 1825.

G **Extract from a description of the opening of the Stockton to Darlington Railway, 27 September 1825, published in 'The Scots Magazine'.**

"On Tuesday . . . the Darlington and Stockton Railway, was formally opened . . . for the use of the public. It is a single railway of twenty-five miles [40 km] in length. . . . The train of carriages was . . . attached to a locomotive engine . . . built by Mr George Stephenson, in the following order: Locomotive engine, with the engineer (Mr Stephenson) and assistants; tender, with coals and water; next, six wagons loaded with coals and flour; then an elegant covered coach, with the committee and . . . proprietors of the railway; then twenty-one wagons . . . for passengers; and, last of all six wagons loaded with coals. . . . At Darlington the whole inhabitants of the town were out to witness the procession . . . all along the line people crowded the fields on each side. . . ."

5 *Read Source* G .

a Which event is described in Source G ?

b The engine was called Locomotion No. 1. Suggest reasons why this was an appropriate name.

c Why was it necessary to carry coal and water in the tender, immediately behind the engine?

d Comment briefly on the principal commodities (goods) carried on the first journey of the Stockton to Darlington Railway.

e What were the main disadvantages of a single track railway?

Linking evidence

6 Sources E , F and G have a common theme. What is it and when did the event take place?

7 Does the written Source G help in any way to establish the accuracy and reliability of the picture Sources E and F ?

8 What evidence can you find to indicate that Sources E and F show the same scene but from a different angle or viewing point? List all the similarities you can between the two scenes.

9 Are there any differences between the two illustrations?

10 How many of the features described in Source G can you identify in the picture Sources E and F ?

11 Which of the Sources E , F and G , in your opinion, provides the most useful and reliable information for an historian? Give reasons for your answer.

12 In question 4a you estimated the length of the Stockton and Darlington railway. Does your estimate agree with the evidence in Source G ?

13 Compare Sources A and G . What do the dates reveal about the time taken to develop the Stockton to Darlington Railway?

14 Look at the picture Sources (E and F) and read the written Source (G). From the point of view of *either* one of the spectators *or* one of the passengers describe what it might have felt like to view, or travel on an early railway train. (Here are some things for you to think about: speed 10 miles per hour – 16 kilometres; sensation of travelling faster than by horse; standing in an open waggon; reactions and conversation of fellow spectators or passengers.)

13 Gas lighting

A **Comment by Sir Walter Scott on the proposals in the early nineteenth century to light London with gas.**
"A madman is proposing to light London with – what do you think? Why, with smoke!"

C **Extract from a letter to Lady Mary Bennet in 1821.**
"What folly [foolishness] to have a diamond necklace or a Correggio [a painting by the artist of that name], and not light your house with gas! . . . Dear Lady, spend your fortune on gas-apparatus. Better to eat dry bread by the splendour of gas than dine on wild beef with wax candles. . . ."

D **Extract from 'Connections' by James Burke, published in 1983.**
"By 1823 there were 300 miles of mains piping, and by 1850 this had increased to 2000 miles . . . The social effects of the gas were widespread. It made the streets instantly safer at night . . . it . . . made longer factory hours possible, and in consequence production levels rose. The evenings could now be fully used, and the spread of literacy that followed the setting up of workers' institutes increased the sales of books. The new light also gave birth to evening classes . . . great London clubs grew up as evening became, for the first time in history, a time of day when community activity could take place."

B Cartoon drawn in 1815 by George Cruikshank on the introduction of gas lighting.

Questions

1 *Read Source* A .
   a What is the 'smoke' referred to?
   b How do you know that Sir Walter Scott was not in favour of lighting London in this way?

2 *Look at Source* B .
   a What new form of energy is the subject of this cartoon?
   b Why do you think the pavements and roads are being dug up? What are the pipes (1) to be used for?
   c What was this new form of energy first used for?
   d Which people might suffer hardship if the new form of energy becomes widespread (2)?
   e Do you think the cartoonist was a supporter or an opponent of gas lighting?

3 *Read Source* C .
   a Does this Source give the impression that: (i) it was *foolish* to use gas lighting; or (ii) it was *fashionable* to use gas lighting? Explain your reasons.
   b Did the writer of Source C prefer gas or wax candles for lighting the house?
   c Is Source C a statement of *fact* or *opinion*?

4 *Read Source* D .
   a What were the *social* benefits of using gas lamps to light the streets?
   b What evidence in Source D indicates that gas was successful as a new form of energy?
   c What other benefits resulted from the use of gas to provide light?

Linking evidence

5 In what ways does Source C show a different attitude to that expressed in Source A ?

6 Does the way gas lighting is shown in the cartoon (B) support the views expressed in Source A or in Source C ?

7 Which of the Sources A – D is a secondary source? Explain how it might be of use to an historian.

8 Before the introduction of gas lighting, streets, homes and workplaces had been lit by candles or oil lamps. How do you imagine some people would have felt about the new, brighter illumination?

9 What does the evidence in Sources A and B tell you about the attitude of some people towards new ideas?

10 What drawbacks did the use of gas have for some people (Source B)?

11 If you had been living in the early nineteenth century would you: (i) have your house fitted with gas lamps; (ii) continue to use oil lamps and candles; or (iii) want more information? Give reasons for your answer.

14 Water supplies and sanitation

A **Extract from the evidence of Robert Baker, District Surgeon, published in the 'Report of the Leeds Board of Health', 3 January 1833.**
"On the 26th [May 1832] . . . the first case of . . . Cholera occurred in the Blue Bell Fold, a small and dirty cul de sac [a street closed at one end], containing about 20 houses, inhabited by poor families . . . on the North side of the river, in an angle between it and an offensive beck or streamlet which conveys the refuse water from numerous mills and dyehouses. . . . The disease . . . spread with considerable rapidity . . . became general in the beginning of July, was at its height in August, and the Board of Health ceased to have reports from its district surgeons on the 12th of November. . . .

. . . amidst a population of 76,000 persons not more than 14 [streets] . . . have . . . common sewers . . . most . . . streets are unsewered, undrained, unpaved . . . in three parallel streets . . . for a population . . . of 386 persons, there are but two single privies [lavatories]. . . ."

B **Extract from a report by Joseph Quick, an engineer with the Southwark Water Company, London, 1844.**
"*Regular queueing for water*
I have seen as many as from 20 to 50 persons with pails waiting round one or two stand-pipes . . . quarrelling for the turn, the strongest pushing forward, and the pails, after they are filled, being upset."

C **Extract from the 'Second Report of the Commissioners for Inquiring into the State of Large Towns and Populous Districts', 1845.**
"*Intermittent piped water supplies*
The system of supplying water usually adopted by companies, is to turn it on to the several districts of the town at certain periods of the day, generally two or three times a week."

D **Cartoon by John Leech from 'Punch', c.1850.**

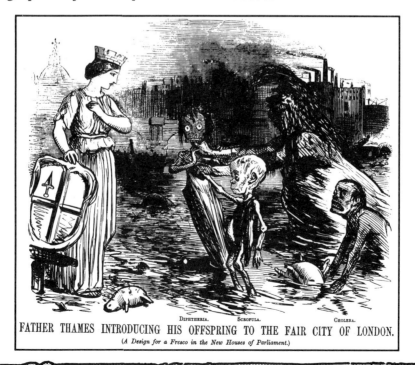

DIPHTHERIA.   SCROFULA.   CHOLERA.
FATHER THAMES INTRODUCING HIS OFFSPRING TO THE FAIR CITY OF LONDON.
(*A Design for a Fresco in the New Houses of Parliament.*)

Questions

1 *Read Source* A .
  a How can you tell that this is a primary source?
  b Where, and in which month, did the first case of cholera occur in Leeds in 1832?
  c Can you suggest reasons why cholera began in the Blue Bell Fold?
  d In which months of the year was the disease at its height? Explain why this was so.
  e Suggest reasons why cholera spread so rapidly.
  f If you had been the District Surgeon in Leeds in 1832–33 what recommendations for improvement for the disposal of sewage and other waste would you have made in your report to the Leeds Board of Health?

2 *Look at Sources* B , C *and* D .
  a These Sources have a common theme. What is it?
  b In what ways might the methods of obtaining water described in Sources B , C and D contribute to the outbreak and spread of epidemic disease?
  c Imagine you had to collect water as shown and described in Sources B , C and D . Think about what would be your priorities for its use. Rearrange the following in order of priority and explain your selections: (i) drinking; (ii) cleaning house; (iii) washing (self); (iv) cooking; (v) swilling down an outside yard or courtway.
  d At which times of the year might it be very difficult to obtain water supplies?
  e Do the Sources B , C and D help you to understand why some people living in the poorer areas of large towns might not be too concerned with personal cleanliness? Explain why.

3 *Look at Source* D
  a Describe the figures which represent (i) Father Thames and (ii) the City of London.
  b What diseases ('offspring') is the River Thames giving to the city of London?
  c Can you suggest why the cartoonist calls the diseases 'offspring' (children) of Father Thames?
  d The River Thames was used for transport. From the evidence in the cartoon can you suggest *two* other uses of the river to the population of London?
  e The cartoonist is trying to influence public opinion. (i) What is the message the cartoonist is trying to get across to people? (ii) What do you think people would feel on seeing this cartoon?
  f What does the cartoon tell us about the attitude of the public towards the use of the river?

Linking evidence

4 Why might the cholera epidemics of 1831–32 (32,000 deaths) and 1847–48 (53,000 deaths) encourage the Government and middle classes to accept the need for improvement in public health?

5 How might the Sources in this section be useful for a reformer or Member of Parliament seeking to improve public health?

6 Using information from the Sources, write a letter (dated 1 January 1851) to a newspaper demanding improvements in water supplies and sanitation for the town you live in.

7 Given all the evidence pointing to the need for improved water supplies and sanitation, suggest why some people were reluctant that the Government and Parliament should take action?

15.1 Changes in the Poor Law

A **Extract from the 'Report of the Commissioners for enquiring into the Administration of the Poor Laws', 1834.**
"We recommend . . . First, that except as to medical attendance . . . all relief to able-bodied persons or families, otherwise than in well-rcgulated workhouses, shall be declared unlawful and shall cease. We recommend the appointment of a Central Board to control the administration of the Poor Laws, with such Assistant Commissioners as may be found requisite [necessary]; and that the Commissioners be empowered to enforce regulations for the government of workhouses, and the nature and amount of the relief to be given, and the labour to be exacted in them, and that such regulations shall be uniform throughout the country. . . ."

B **A contemporary cartoon showing one view of the changes in the Poor Law.**

C **Extract from 'History, Gazetteer and Directory of Suffolk, 1844' by W. White.**
". . . in Suffolk twenty large WORKHOUSES, having accommodation for 7,000 paupers; but in summer, they have seldom as many as 3,000, and in winter, rarely more than 5,000 inmates. Eight of the largest are . . . 'Houses of Industry', built in the latter part of the last century, under Gilbert's and local Acts . . . ten large new workhouses have been erected and the old ones have been enlarged . . . to adapt them to the new system . . . The out-door able bodied paupers were very numerous in . . . agricultural counties, owing to the . . . mal-administration of the old poor law, which was eating . . . into the heart of the nation, pauperising the labourers, taking away the motive and the reward of industry. . . ."

AS THEY WERE.   POOR LAWS   AS THEY ARE.

D **Extract from the evidence of Charles Lewis, a labourer, quoted in the 'Report of the Select Committee relating to Andover Union'.**

"Q *What work were you employed about when you were in the workhouse?*
A I was employed breaking bones.
Q *Were other men engaged in the same work?*
A Yes.
Q *Was that the only employment you had?*
A That was the only employment I had at the time I was there.
Q *Was the smell very bad?*
A Very bad.
Q *How did you break them?*
A We had a large bar to break them with.
Q *During the time you were so employed, did you ever see any men gnaw anything or eat anything from those bones?*
A I have seen them eat marrow out of the bones.
Q *Did they state why they did it?*
A I really believe they were hungry.
Q *Did you see any of the men gnaw the meat from the bones?*
A Yes.
Q *And when a fresh set of bones came in, did they keep a sharp look-out for the best?*
A Yes."

Questions

1 *Read Source* **A** .
  a What recommendations did the Commissioners make concerning poor relief?
  b What was to happen to the able-bodied poor who were dependent on the parish for support?
  c The Commissioners argued that conditions in the workhouse should be worse than that of the lowest-paid labourers outside the workhouse. What does this suggest about the attitude of the Commissioners towards those who were claiming poor relief?

2 *Look at Source* **B** .
  a What is the subject of the cartoon and what scenes are shown?
  b What differences does the cartoonist show between the workhouses 'as they were' and 'as they are'?
  c How does the cartoonist suggest that paupers were worse off after the New Poor Law came into operation in 1834? What does the right-hand scene suggest about the attitude of the cartoonist towards the New Poor Law?
  d Was the cartoonist 'biased' in the way he presented the subject or did he attempt to give a 'balanced' view? Give reasons for your answer.

3 *Read Source* **C** .
  a How do you explain the fact that in Suffolk, a farming county, there were fewer paupers in summer than in winter?
  b Under Gilbert's Act of 1782 local parishes were allowed to join together to set up a workhouse for the poor. What was the effect of that Act in Suffolk?
  c What changes occurred in the provision for the poor in Suffolk between 1834 when the 'new system' was introduced and 1844?
  d Who were the 'outdoor able bodied paupers'?
  e According to Source **C** what were the main defects of the old poor law?

4 *Look at Source* **D** .
  a Suggest why the evidence given in Source **D** is sometimes described as a 'scandal'.
  b What work was carried out by the inmates of Andover workhouse?
  c What were the inmates driven to do out of hunger?
  d Why might this evidence be useful to those who opposed the New Poor Law?

15.2   Changes in the Poor Law

E Extract from 'Oliver Twist' by Charles Dickens, first published in 1838.

". . . they . . . issued three meals of thin gruel a day, with an onion twice a week, and half a roll on Sundays. . . .

The room in which the boys were fed, was a large stone hall, with a copper [a large vessel for boiling things in] at one end; out of which the master, dressed in an apron for the purpose, and assisted by one or two women, ladled the gruel at meal-times. . . . Oliver Twist and his companions suffered the tortures of slow starvation for three months. . . . A council was held; lots were cast who should walk up to the master after supper that evening and ask for more; and it fell to Oliver Twist. . . .

'Please, Sir, I want some more'. . . .

The master was a fat healthy man; . . . He gazed in . . . astonishment on the small rebel . . . and then clung for support to the copper. The assistants were paralysed wth wonder; the boys with fear. . . ."

G Extract from 'The Northern Star', 10 March 1838.

"*Address of the Anti-Poor Law Association Committee at Huddersfield*

FELLOW RATE PAYERS

The time has come for you to give a practical demonstration of your hatred to the new Starvation Law. Recollect . . . the 25th of March is the day . . . for the election of new Guardians . . . it will depend upon your exertions, whether you will allow men to be elected . . . who are the tools of the three Commissioners in carrying out their diabolical schemes for starving the poor, reducing the labourers' wages, and robbing you the rate-payers of . . . control . . . over your money . . . and township affairs; or will you elect men of character and of humanity, whose . . . independent spirit will scorn to submit to the three-headed monster of Somerset House [the administrators of the new Poor Law]. . . ."

F Illustration by the cartoonist George Cruikshank of the scene in 'Oliver Twist' in which Oliver asks for more food.

5 *Read Source* E .
   a Why did Oliver Twist ask for more food?
   b What was the reaction to Oliver's request?
   c Why do you think the other boys were afraid?
   d Does the extract support or disapprove of the conditions resulting from the working of the New Poor Law? Give reasons for your answer.
   e What is Source E ? How useful is this type of evidence to an historian? Why might this type of evidence present problems for an historian?

6 *Look at Sources* E *and* F .
   a How accurately do you think the artist has illustrated the extract from *Oliver Twist* (Source E)?
   b Study the illustration and write down all the phrases in the extract (Source E) which are shown in the scene. (*Example*: the copper at one end.) Give at least 5 examples.
   c If you had drawn the 'short straw' instead of Oliver, how might you have felt at that time? Describe your feelings in not less than 50 words using the following pairs of words: I feared; I hoped; I thought; I believed.
   d Would Dickens' book, *Oliver Twist*, be welcomed more by the supporters than by the opponents of the 1834 Poor Law Amendment Act? Give reasons for your answer.

7 *Read Source* G .
   a To whom was the speech made?
   b Why did the Anti-Poor Law Association oppose the 1834 Poor Law Amendment Act?
   c According to Source G what was the real intention of the new Poor Law?
   d How were the ratepayers urged to show their hatred of the new Poor Law?

Linking evidence

8 From the evidence in this chapter state two important *results* of the 1834 Poor Law Amendment Act.

9 It is clear that not everyone opposed the workhouses. Using the evidence in this chapter explain why some people approved of the effects of the new Poor Law.

10 The *Quarterly Review* stated of the book *Oliver Twist* that it was 'directed against the Poor Law and the workhouse system . . . with much unfairness. The abuses which he ridicules are not only exaggerated, but in nineteen cases out of twenty do not at all exist'. Would the Sources B , C , D and G tend to support the views of Charles Dickens or those of the *Quarterly Review*?

11 From the evidence in Sources A – G do you consider that the new Poor Law was (i) deliberately harsh to dissuade the poor from seeking poor relief or (ii) designed to operate a more efficient system of poor relief than that under the old Poor Law? Give your reasons.

12 Sources D , E , F and G are very different in *form* and *content*. Which do you consider most effective in arousing public opposition to the new Poor Law? Give reasons.

13 Sources D – G all provide evidence against the new Poor Law. Does this mean that they are of no use to an historian as Sources to be used in studying the effects of the 1834 Act?

14 Source B is a cartoon. Source A is an extract from an official Report. Does this mean that Source B would be less useful than Source A to an historian studying the poor law? Explain.

16   Prisons – revenge or reform?

A Elizabeth Fry reading the bible to prisoners in Newgate, 1816.

B The opinion of Elizabeth Fry.
"Punishment is not for revenge, but to lessen crime and reform the criminal. . . ."

C The opinion of Rev. Sydney Smith.
"Prisons are really meant to keep the multitude in order, and to be a terror to evil-doers. . . . There must be a great deal of solitude; coarse food; a dress of shame; hard, incessant, irksome eternal labour; a planned and regulated and unrelenting exclusion of happiness and comfort. . . ."

D Extract from the 'Annual Return to the Secretary of State . . . the County Gaol (Jail) and House of Correction at Maidstone', 1840.
"Q   *How are prisoners sentenced to Hard Labour employed?*
  A   Male prisoners sentenced to Hard Labour are employed at the Treading Wheel, and in the Manufacture of Sacking, Mat Making, Shoe Making and Shoe Mending . . . Females sentenced to Hard Labour are employed at the Treading Wheel, in Washing, Ironing and Needle Work.
Q   *What are the Hours of Labour?*
A   When the day light admits, the prisoners commence work at six o'clock in the morning and leave work at half past five in the evening, deducting . . . half an hour for Breakfast, an hour for Dinner, and the time required for Chapel. . . .
Q   *What is the nature of the punishment inflicted and for what offences are prisoners so punished?*
A   Whipping. In Irons, Confinement in Dark and Solitary Cells and Stoppages of Diet. The offences for which punished . . . Attempting to Escape, Refusing to work, Pilfering, Using profane language, Quarreling, Having prohibited articles in their possession, Talking or other misbehaviour at Work and Misbehaviour in Chapel."

E An artist's view of prisoners walking a treadmill.

Questions

1 *Look at Source* A .
  a What is the setting for the picture?
  b The artist has distinguished between the visitors (left) and the prisoners (right) in a number of ways. List as many differences as you can see.
  c From the evidence in Sources A – E , would you say that: (i) the people in the painting had been deliberately 'posed' by the artist to create a favourable impression of Elizabeth Fry; or (ii) the scene was typical of a scene in Newgate prison at that time? Give reasons for your answer.
  d Why might an historian wish to consult other evidence of conditions in Newgate prison before making use of Source A ?
  e Choose *either* one of the visitors *or* one of the prisoners shown in the picture. Describe in a paragraph what he or she might be thinking and feeling at that time.
  f Can you suggest why Elizabeth Fry might want her work in prisons to be observed by visitors? How might it benefit (i) her work; and (ii) the prisoners?

Linking evidence

2 Reform or revenge? From the evidence in Sources A and B , which did Elizabeth Fry believe should be the main purpose of the penal system?

3 How does the view of Rev. Sydney Smith (Source C) on the purpose of the penal system differ from that of Elizabeth Fry (Source B)? What conditions did Smith suggest as a means of deterring 'evil-doers'?

4 **a** Using Sources D and E describe in your own words how a treadmill worked.
  b What feature on the top of the building (Source E) shows that the activity served no other useful purpose than 'exercising' and 'punishing' the prisoners?
  c Occasionally, a treadmill might turn a corn mill. Do you think it might have made a difference to the prisoners if their labours were used for a practical purpose, and not simply as punishment?
  d Which Source (D or E) provides the most useful evidence about the treadmill system? Explain why.

5 Would the author of Source C be more likely to approve the scene shown in Source A or the one shown in Source E ? Give reasons for your answer.

17   The new police force

A **Extract from a letter from Sir Robert Peel, Home Secretary, to the Prime Minister, the Duke of Wellington, 29 May 1829.**

"I send you the report of the Committee . . . on the Police of the Metropolis [London]. In 1822 there were 2,539 committals . . . in 1828, 3,516. . . .

The paper marked A contains a list of parishes in which the watch . . . is defective. . . .

The paper marked B contains a list of parishes, in the immediate vicinity of London, in which there is absolutely no watch at all. My Bill enables the Secretary of State to abolish gradually the existing watch arrangements, and to substitute in their room a police force . . . under the control of two magistrates. I propose to substitute the new police gradually for the old one . . . to begin . . . with . . . the City of Westminster, and gradually to extend the police district. . . ."

B **Extract from the Act of 1829 setting up a new police force in London.**

Be it therefore enacted that it shall be lawful for His Majesty to cause a new Police Office to be established in the City of Westminster for the more efficient Administration of the Police within . . . the Metropolitan Police District; and a sufficient number of fit and able Men shall be appointed . . . to act as Constables for preserving Peace and preventing Robberies and other Felonies [crimes], and apprehending Offenders against the Peace."

C **Extract from an article in 'The Times', 1830.**

". . . the police have neither swords nor pistols to defend themselves; and recent circumstances suffice to prove that for the preservation of their own lives, to say nothing of the public, the bits of stick with which they are at present provided are anything but an adequate protection. We ourselves have seen nothing of the police but exemplary courtesy, forbearance and propriety, great willingness to act and, when the occasion calls, to refrain from acting.

D **Extract from the evidence of Samuel Clark, given to the Select Committee on the Conduct of the Police, 1833.**

Q   *What did you see on this occasion?*

A   I was a witness to the brutality of the police . . . I saw them use all the violence they possibly could.

Q   *Where were you standing?*

A   At my door. I saw a mob of people rushing from the field towards my house, and the police after the people, striking everyone.

Q   *Do you think that since the police has been established there has been better order kept in your neighbourhood than there was before?*

A   I think there might be with a little better management. I had always been a supporter of the police until this misconduct, but it made me feel that I shall never like the police any more."

E **Cartoonist's view of a police constable or 'Peeler'.**

Questions

1 *Read Source* A .
   a Why might Source A be regarded as a reliable source of evidence by an historian?
   b What evidence can you find that the number of crimes in London (the 'Metropolis') was growing rapidly in the 1820s?
   c What changes did Sir Robert Peel want to make and how did he plan to do it?
   d The 'New Police' became known as 'Bobbies' or 'Peelers'. Can you suggest why?

2 *Read Source* B .
   a What was the purpose of the 1829 Act?
   b Where was the new police system to be set up and what were to be the duties of the constables?

3 *Read Source* C .
   a Why did he consider that the police were unprotected?
   b What were the 'bits of stick' which were provided for each policeman? Are they still carried and used by policemen today?
   c Do you think the opinions expressed in Source C are *well balanced* or *biased*? Explain.

4 *Read Source* D .
   a Source D is an extract from the evidence given to a Select Committee. What was the Committee inquiring into?
   b How was Samuel Clark involved in the event he described? What was his view of the conduct of the police? Quote from the Source to support your answer.
   c Why had Samuel Clark's attitude towards the police changed?
   d Give one *fact* and one *opinion* from Samuel Clark's evidence.
   e 'Source D is a reliable source because it was given in evidence by an eyewitness to the event.' Do you agree or disagree with this statement? Explain why.
   f How might the Select Committee try to check the reliability of the evidence of Samuel Clark?

5 *Look at Source* E .
   a How does the cartoonist try to suggest that the police were no better than criminals?
   b Would you consider Source E to be a balanced piece of evidence? Explain your answer.

Linking evidence

6 Does Source D support or contradict the view expressed in Source C ?

7 Does the view of the 'New Police' presented by the cartoonist in Source E support those expressed in Source C or that given in evidence in Source D ?

8 Sources B , C , D and E all relate to the early years of the new police force. How do you account for such differing attitudes being held by people living at the same time?

9 'Source E is a cartoon. Source B is an extract from an Act of Parliament. Source B would therefore be more valuable to an historian than Source E .' Do you agree or disagree with this statement? Say why.

18.1 Peterloo, 1819

A Extract from 'History of Manchester and Salford' by F. A. Bruton, published in 1927.

"Into the open space [St Peter's Field] . . . the Reformers . . . poured . . . in excellent order . . . with bands playing, silk banners flying . . . and girls in white dancing and singing . . . Four or five abreast they marched, their banners . . . proclaiming . . . 'Universal Suffrage', 'Annual Parliaments', 'Vote by Ballot', 'No Corn Laws', et cetera . . . The National Anthem was sung at twelve-thirty . . . Arrived at the hustings [platform], Hunt [Henry Hunt, the leading speaker at the meeting] . . . taking off his white hat, which had become the symbol of Radicalism [the movement for Parliamentary reform] . . . began his speech, facing an impressive crowd of some sixty thousand, consisting of men, women, and children.

The magistrates . . . who had . . . sat till midnight without being able to decide upon any definite plan of action . . . at length made up their minds, a warrant for the arrest of the speakers was handed to the Deputy Constable, Nadin. . . . He declared that the three hundred special constables at his disposal were not a sufficient force to enable him to execute it. The magistrates therefore despatched mounted messengers . . . for the Manchester Yeomanry, and . . . for the Hussars and the Cheshires. A few minutes later, the Manchester Yeomanry . . . halting for a moment in great disorder, for they had no command of their horses, made a dash for the hustings, striking with their swords as they entered the crowd . . . untrained . . . they were soon . . . hopelessly entangled. . . .

. . . 'What am I to do?' asked Lieut.-Colonel L'Estrange [of the Hussars], looking . . . at . . . Mr Hulton [chairman of the magistrates] . . . 'Good God! Sir,' . . . 'don't you see they are attacking the yeomanry? Disperse the meeting.'. . .

. . . The Hussars . . . beating back the crowd with the flats of their swords, and sometimes . . . with the edges also . . . swept the square . . . so rapidly . . . that in ten minutes those . . . watching from upper windows . . . looked down upon an empty space . . . save for human beings lying in heaps, sabred, crushed, and trampled. . . ."

B A section of a contemporary plan of St Peter's Field (Peterloo), 1819.

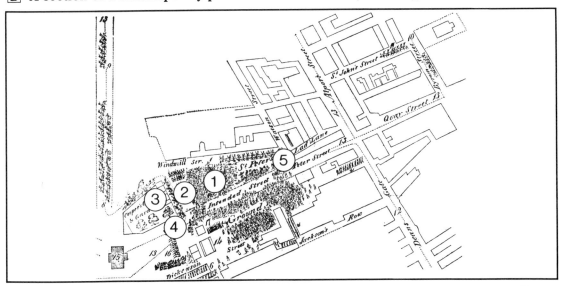

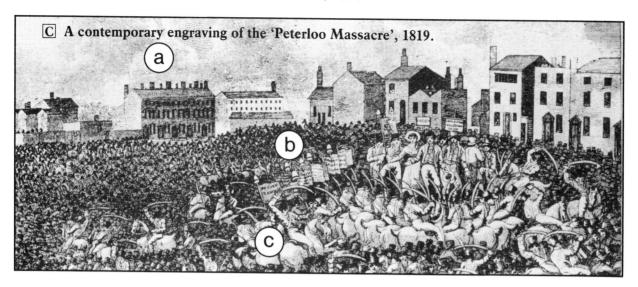

C A contemporary engraving of the 'Peterloo Massacre', 1819.

Questions

1 *Read Source* A .

a Source A was written many years after the events it describes. Does this limit its use to an historian?

b What kinds of reforms were the people who attended the meeting hoping to achieve?

c What evidence in the extract might be used to support the view that: (i) the crowd were reformers rather than revolutionaries; (ii) the organizers of the meeting did not expect that there would be any violence; (iii) the crowd were patriotic; (iv) the Yeomanry were inexperienced horsemen? Give one example in each case.

d Why were the Manchester Yeomanry and, later, the Hussars sent into the crowd? Give one *cause* and one *effect* of the decision.

e Is there any evidence to indicate that: (i) the people in the crowd were armed; (ii) the Yeomanry and the Hussars were armed?

f What does the extract tell you about the attitude of the author of Source A ?

2 *Look at Sources* A , B *and* C .

a Source B shows the banners and Caps of Liberty arranged at 1. Which letter in the engraving (Source C) shows that feature?

b Source B shows a double row of special constables at 2. How many constables were present (Source A)?

c Source B shows the house where the magistrates met at 3. Which letter in the engraving (Source C) indicates that feature? What did the magistrates ask the Deputy Constable to do, and what did he reply (Source A)?

d Source B shows the Manchester Yeomanry at 4. What did the magistrates order them to do (Source A)?

e Source B shows the Manchester Yeomanry charging the crowd at 5. Which letter in the engraving (Source C) indicates that feature? What happened to the Manchester Yeomanry when they entered the crowd, and why (Source A)?

f From the evidence in Sources A and C describe the part played by women and girls in the meeting at St Peter's Field.

g Do you think the engraver of Source C was a supporter or opponent of the reformers?

h In what ways might the use of Sources B and C increase the usefulness of Source A for an historian?

18.2   Peterloo, 1819

D **Extract from evidence given at the trial of Henry Hunt in 1820 by John Walker, an attorney.**

"I heard Mr Hunt desire the people . . . to keep silence and if their enemies would not keep order to put them down and keep them down or something to that effect. In my judgement it was not possible to penetrate the crowd near the hustings without absolute force. They formed a solid body. . . . There were upwards of 50,000 persons present. The division I saw marched to the ground in military manner. . . . The crowd consisted of the lower class of people. To so assemble was designed to overawe, to intimidate, and to create fear and alarm in the minds of the people of the town. This was the impression of my mind. I felt fear and dread as I thought it would create a disturbance."

E **Extract from 'An Exposure of the Calumnies Circulated by the Enemies of Social Order' by F. Philips, published in November 1819.**

". . . I mixed with the crowd . . . and was at one time within twenty-five yards [22 metres] of the hustings. . . . Although no direct affront was offered me, the observations, boldly and tauntingly made, convinced me of the revolutionary tendency of the meeting, and that they were confident of eventually overturning the Government. . . . The Yeomanry . . . proceeded at a slow pace, it appeared to me, in file; but from the numbers before me, I could not see distinctly. I was alarmed for their safety. . . . Whilst near me, I did not see a sword used, and . . . if the crowd had given way to them, no cuts would have been given; a great dust arose when they quickened their speed, so that I could not distinguish all that passed, but certainly I did not see one person struck with the sabre. . . ."

F **Extract from the evidence of Rev. E. Stanley, quoted in 'Three Accounts of Peterloo' edited by F. Bruton.**

"I heard the sound of a horn and immediately the Manchester Yeomanry appeared . . . and galloped towards the hustings. . . . Their sabres glistened in the air. . . . As the cavalry approached the . . . people . . . used their utmost efforts to escape; but so closely were they pressed in opposite directions by the soldiers, the special constables, the position of the hustings and their own immense numbers, that immediate escape was impossible.

The Manchester Yeomanry had already taken possession of the hustings, when the Cheshire Yeomanry entered on my left . . . the Fifteenth Dragoons appeared nearly at the same moment. . . . They then pressed forward, crossing the avenue of constables, which opened to let them through, and set their course towards the Manchester Yeomanry. The people were now in a state of utter rout and confusion . . . I saw nothing that gave me an idea of resistance. . . ."

G **Extract from an article written by a Special Correspondent of 'The Times'.**

". . . As soon as Hunt and Johnson had jumped from the waggon (to surrender) a cry was made by the cavalry, 'Have at their flags'. They immediately dashed not only at the flags which were in the wagon, but those which were posted among the crowd, cutting most indiscriminately to the right and left in order to get at them. This set the people running in all directions, and it was not till this act had been committed that any brick-bats were hurled at the military. From that moment the Manchester Yeomanry Cavalry lost all command of temper. A man within five yards [4·5 metres] of us had his nose completely taken off by a blow of a sabre. . . ."

Linking evidence

3 Sources D, E, F and G all provide evidence from people who were present at the event.
  a Quoting from these Sources, give three examples of contradictory evidence.
  b How do you account for such widely differing views of the same event?

4 List all the words or phrases in Sources D, E, F and G which might make you doubt the accuracy of some of the evidence given (*Example*: 'or something to that effect' (Source D)).

5 Which Source in your opinion, provides: (i) the *most* reliable evidence; (ii) the *least* reliable evidence? Give reasons for your choice in each case.

6 From the evidence in Sources A – G do you consider:
  (i)   that the size of the crowd *was* or *was not* a threat to law and order;
  (ii) that the crowd was *peaceable* or *unruly*;
  (iii) that Henry Hunt *should* or *should not* have been arrested in front of a large crowd;
  (iv) that the Manchester Yeomanry *should* or *should not* have been sent into the crowd;
  (v)   that the crowd *resisted* or *gave way* before the advance of the Manchester Yeomanry;
  (vi) that the Manchester Yeomanry *galloped* or *proceeded at a slow pace* through the crowd;
  (vii) that the Manchester Yeomanry *did* or *did not* cut at the crowd with their sabres?

7 From all the evidence given, can you suggest why so many people were killed or injured at St Peter's Field?

8 '. . . The days before the meeting were full of tension and suspicion on behalf of the authorities. The legality of the coming meeting was questioned. . . .' (P. Gregg, *Social and Economic History of Britain* (1965)). In your opinion should: (i) Hunt and the organizers have cancelled the meeting; (ii) the magistrates have banned the meeting; or (iii) the meeting have gone ahead as planned?

9 In 1868 the Manchester Liberal Party stated that: 'The meeting was perfectly legal and had its promoters and the people been left to themselves it would, in all probability, have dispersed in quietness and peace. . . .' How far do you agree with this statement? Quote from the evidence to support your answer.

10 '. . . The magistrates . . . seem to have been perplexed between the resolution to maintain . . . order . . . and their fear of acting prematurely. . . .' In your opinion how far did the indecisiveness of the magistrates contribute to the massacre at St Peter's Field?

11 If you could have interviewed *three* of the people present at St Peter's Field on 16 August 1819, who would you have chosen and what questions would you have asked each of them?

12 'No *single* factor was to blame for the events at St Peter's Field, rather it was a *combination* of factors.'
  a Do you *agree* or *disagree* with this statement?
  b Who or what do *you* blame for the massacre which came to be known as Peterloo?

19.1 Parliamentary reform

A A cartoon of the consequences of voting against your landlord.

Freedom & Purity of Election!!! Showing the Necessity of Reform in the Close Boroughs.

B Cartoon by George Cruikshank 1831.

Questions

1 *Look at Source* A .

a Some of the people shown in Source A are being turned out (evicted) of their houses. Can you explain why?

b Those evicted had voted 'according to conscience'. Does this mean that they had: (i) voted as the landlord had instructed; (ii) refused to vote; (iii) voted for the candidate of their own choice?

c Why did the landlord, who owned the houses, object to his tenants voting 'according to conscience'?

d The landlord knew how his tenants had voted because elections were conducted 'openly'. Can you suggest a reform in the method of voting which would protect such tenants?

e In what ways might this cartoon have been useful for reformers and politicians seeking to reform the electoral system? What changes might they have recommended?

f Choose one of the characters in Source A and describe how he or she might have felt at the time.

2 *Look at Source* B .

a Can you explain the connection between the wheel (1) containing the names of the rotten and pocket boroughs controlled by the great landowners and aristocracy, the 'Grinding Machine' (2) worked by the wheel which represents the House of Commons (St Stephens) and the flow of jobs, pensions and public money (3) which the great landowners, their families and friends are enjoying?

b One of the most corrupt of the rotten boroughs was Boroughbridge in Yorkshire, where there were a handful of electors and where the owner, the Duke of Newcastle, controlled the election of two MPs. How has the cartoonist drawn attention to Boroughbridge?

c The cartoonist shows the 'System' being supported by the armed forces (4). What symbols has the cartoonist used?

d What was the attitude of the cartoonist towards the Parliamentary system? Was he *for* or *against* Parliamentary reform? Explain your answer.

3 *Look at Sources* A *and* B .

a Sources A and B have a similar theme and a similar form. (i) What is the theme of the Sources? (ii) What form do the Sources take?

b Do you think the people who produced Sources A and B were in favour of or opposed to parliamentary reform?

c Do you think that the Sources A and B are *fair* or *biased*? Explain.

d In your opinion, which of the two Sources, A or B , is most effective in arguing the case for parliamentary reform. Explain why, and support your answer with evidence from the Sources.

e What questions should an historian ask before making use of cartoons?

f Using the evidence in Sources A and B , write a letter to an MP setting out the case for the reform of Parliament.

19.2   Parliamentary reform

C Extract from a speech by Sir Robert Inglis, MP, on 1 March 1831, quoted in 'Hansard'.

". . . there is, so far as I know, no evidence that our House was ever selected upon any principle of a Representation of population . . . the House of Commons . . . is the most complete representation of the interests of the people, which was ever assembled in any age or country. It is the only constituent body that ever existed, which comprehends within itself, those who can urge the wants and defend the claims of the landed, the commercial, the professional classes of the country; those who are bound to uphold the prerogatives of the Crown, the privileges of the nobility, the interests of the lower classes, the rights and liberties of the whole people."

D Extract from a speech by Lord Palmerston on 3 March 1831, quoted in Hansard.

". . . there were five great . . . blemishes, which it was necessary to remove. . . . The first . . . was the system of nomination by the patrons of boroughs; the second . . . corruption . . . among the lower classes, when their votes became necessary to the higher; the third, the absence of . . . adequate . . . representation with respect to the great manufacturing . . . towns; the fourth, the great expense of elections: and the fifth, the very unequal . . . distribution of the power of voting among the middle and lower classes. . . .

The object the Government had in view in framing the Bill was, first, to give Representatives to the great manufacturing towns; next, to add to the respectability of the electors; and then to increase the number of those who claim to enjoy the right of choosing their Representatives . . . by throwing open the closed boroughs to the inhabitants of the surrounding parishes . . . and making it impossible for any individual to control them. . . ."

E Extract from a speech by a Whig, T. B. Macaulay, in the House of Commons on 2 March 1831.

". . . I am opposed to universal suffrage, because . . . it would produce a destructive revolution. I support this plan . . . it is our best security against a revolution . . . we may exclude those whom it is necessary to exclude, we must admit those whom it may be safe to admit . . . it is not by mere numbers, but by property and intelligence, that the nation ought to be governed. Yet . . . we exclude . . . great masses of property and intelligence. . . . We drive over to the side of revolution those whom we shut out from power.

History is full of revolutions, produced by causes similar to those which are now operating in England. A portion of the community which had been of no account expands and becomes strong. It demands a place in the system, suited to its present power. If this is granted, all is well. If this is refused, then comes the struggle between the young energy of one class and the ancient privileges of another. Such is the struggle which the middle classes are maintaining against . . . aristocracy."

F Extract from a letter from the Duke of Wellington to the Tory politician and writer, John Croker, March 1833.

"The revolution is made; power is transferred from one class of society, the gentlemen of England, to another class of society, the shopkeepers . . . a new democratic influence has been introduced into elections, the copy-holders and free-holders and lease-holders residing in towns . . . are everywhere a formidably active party against the aristocratic influence of the Landed Gentry. . . . The mischief of the reform is that whereas democracy prevailed heretofore only in some places, it now prevails everywhere. . . . Believe me ever yours most sincerely,

Wellington"

4 *Read Source* C .

  a Source C is a primary source. How do you know?

  b According to Source C , were members of Parliament selected to: (i) represent the population; or (ii) represent the interests of the population? Can you explain the difference between (i) and (ii)?

  c Was the author of Source C satisfied with the system of representation?

  d How might the author be involved in attempts to reform Parliament? Would he be in favour of the Bill to reform the House of Commons introduced by the Whig Government in 1831?

5 *Read Source* D .

  a Lord Palmerston was a leading member of the Whig Government which introduced the Reform Bill in 1831. What did he believe to be the defects of the existing Parliamentary system?

  b What were the main aims of the Whig Government in introducing the Reform Bill?

6 *Read Source* E .

  a Why was the author of Source E opposed to universal suffrage (votes for all adult males)?

  b Was he for or against the Reform Bill the Whig Government was proposing? Explain his attitude.

  c Which class of people did he consider to be excluded from the Parliamentary system? Why did he believe that class should be given 'a place in the system'?

  d What did he fear might happen if the middle classes were refused 'a place in the system'?

7 *Read Source* F .

  a What type of source is Source F ?

  b What is the subject of the extract?

  c The Reform Act had been passed by Parliament in 1832. (i) Was the Duke of Wellington in favour of the changes? (ii) What did he consider to be the effects of the Act?

  d What were Wellington's views on democracy?

Linking evidence

8 Which of the Sources D – F express doubts about reforming the Parliamentary system?

9 What does the evidence in Sources C – F tell you about the attitude of some people towards the lower classes?

10 Explain in your own words what the Whigs thought was wrong with the Parliamentary system before its reform in 1832.

11 Are Sources C , E and F statements of *fact* or *opinion*? Give your reasons in each case.

12 Which of the Sources C – F supports the views of the cartoonists (Source A + B)?

13 In what ways does Source E show a different attitude to that expressed in Source C ?

14 Sources C , D and E were all written in March 1831. How do you account for such differing views being held at the same time in history?

15 The author of Source E was a Whig who supported the Reform Act. The author of Source F was a Tory who opposed the Reform Act. Despite their differences on some matters they agreed on one issue. What was it?

20 The Chartists

A **Extract from a chartist Petition to Parliament, drafted on 28 February 1837.**
"Your petitioners [the chartists] earnestly pray your Honourable House *to enact the following as the law of these realms.* . . .

1 EQUAL REPRESENTATION. That the United Kingdom be divided into 200 electoral districts . . . and that each district do send a representative to Parliament.

2 UNIVERSAL SUFFRAGE. That every person producing proof of his being 21 years of age . . . shall be entitled to have his name registered as a voter. . . .

3 ANNUAL PARLIAMENTS. That a general election do take place on the 24th of June in each year. . . .

4 NO PROPERTY QUALIFICATIONS. That there shall be no property qualifications for members. . . .

5 VOTE BY BALLOT. That each voter must vote in the parish in which he resides . . . and that a temporary place be fitted up in each parish church for the purpose of *secret voting*. . . .

6 . . . PAYMENTS TO MEMBERS . . . every member shall be paid quarterly out of the public treasury £400 a year. . . .

B **Extract from 'The Annual Register', 1848.**
"The 10th of April was the day which the disciples of physical force, organised under the banner of Chartism, had announced for a grand display of their strength and numbers; a demonstration by which it was intended to overawe the Government into a concession of their demands . . . But . . . without a blow struck, or a drop of blood shed, nay without the appearance of a single soldier in the streets of London . . . peace and order were maintained, and the . . . demonstration passed off quietly and safely. The result was . . . to strengthen the cause of constitutional liberty. . . ."

C **Extract from 'The Greville Memoirs', published in 1852.**
"April . . . 1848. Monday passed off with surprising quiet, and it was considered a most satisfactory demonstration on the part of the Government, and the peaceable and loyal part of the community. The Chartist movement was contemptible.

In the morning . . . everybody was on the alert; the parks were closed; our office was fortified, a barricade of Council Registers was erected in the accessible room on the ground floor, and all our guns were taken down to be used in defence of the building. However, at about twelve o'clock crowds came streaming along Whitehall, going northward, and it was announced that all was over. The intended tragedy was rapidly changed into a ludicrous farce."

D **Cartoon which appeared in 'Punch' after the Chartist meeting on Kennington Common on 10 April 1848. The caption read 'A physical force Chartist arming for the fight that never was'.**

Questions

1 *Read Source* A .
  a What is Source A and to whom was it presented?
  b Who were the 'petitioners'?
  c What was the 'Honourable House'?
  d What were the petitioners asking for?
  e Does the wording of the petition give the impression that the Chartists wanted *all* the people over 21 years of age to have the vote? Explain your answer.
  f Do you consider that the demands made in the Chartist petition were reasonable or not? Explain your answer.
  g Were any of the demands of the Chartists impractical? Explain why.

2 *Look at Sources* B , C *and* D .
  a Sources B , C and D are all connected with an event which took place in April 1848. What was it?
  b There were two main groups within the Chartist movement, the *moral force* Chartists and the *physical force* Chartists. The *moral force* Chartists hoped to achieve their aims by peaceful means. What means do you think the *physical force* Chartists were prepared to use?
  c Do Sources B and C agree with one another in their views of the events of 10 April 1848?
  d In April 1848 London was ringed by troops under the command of the Duke of Wellington to prevent any trouble during the Chartist demonstration. Which of the Sources suggests that there was a *serious* threat of violence in the minds of some people?
  e Faced with the possibility of a clash with the troops, the Chartist leaders called off their planned march to Parliament. Did the authorities regard the Chartist demonstration as a *success* or a *failure*? Quote from Sources B and C to support your answer.
  f The author of Source C described the Chartist demonstration as 'contemptible' and a 'ludicrous farce'. In what ways does the cartoonist (Source D) try to ridicule the *physical force* Chartists?
  g The cartoon (Source D) was drawn after the meeting on 10 April 1848. What is the cartoon trying to show?
  h What does the cartoon tell us about the attitude of some people towards the Chartists?
  i What kinds of people does the cartoonist suggest might belong to the *physical force* Chartists?
  j Do you think the cartoonist was a supporter or an opponent of *physical force* Chartism?

Linking evidence

3 Which of the Sources A – D do you consider to be most biased? Explain.

4 Source C was written by someone who opposed the Chartists. How do you think a Chartist taking part in the demonstration on 10 April 1848 might have described the event?

5 The people who went to the meeting on 10 April 1848 were not protesting about *poverty*. They were protesting about not having *the right to vote*. In what ways might the Chartists feel that there was a connection between the two conditions?

6 As a Chartist in April 1848 *before* the petition is presented to Parliament, write a short speech that might have been made at a public meeting in support of the movement. Refer to the purpose of the Chartist movement, your reasons for joining and previous events in the movement.

7 From the evidence provided, can you suggest one *cause* and one *result* of the meeting on 10 April 1848?

21 Co-operative Societies

A **Extract from the 'Rules of the Rochdale Equitable Pioneers'.**

"At the close of the year 1843 . . . a few poor weavers out of employ, and nearly out of food . . . met together to discover what they could do to better their industrial conditions . . . without experience, or knowledge, or funds, they would turn merchants and manufacturers . . . A dozen . . . put down a weekly subscription of twopence [1p] each. . . .

. . . their Society was registered, October 24th, 1844, under the title of the 'Rochdale Equitable Pioneers'. . . . These Pioneers . . . declared thus:- 'The objects . . . of this Society are . . . the improvement of the . . . condition of its members, by raising . . . capital in shares of one pound each, to bring into operation the following plans. . . . The establishment of a Store for the sale of provisions, clothing, etc. The building, purchasing, or erecting a number of houses . . . the manufacture of . . . articles . . . for the employment of such members as may be without employment, or who may be suffering . . . repeated reductions in their wages . . . the Society shall purchase or rent an estate or estates of land, which shall be cultivated by the members who may be out of employment, or whose labour may be badly remunerated."

B **Extract from 'Self-Help by the People: the History of the Rochdale Pioneers' by G. J. Holyoake, published in 1857.**

"The ground floor of a warehouse in Toad Lane was the place selected in which to commence operations . . . obtained upon a lease of three years at £10 per annum . . . commodities [goods] consisted of . . . flour, butter, sugar, and oatmeal . . . after . . . paying for the necessary fixtures, £14 or £15 was all they had to invest in stock . . . on . . . 21st of December, 1844, the 'Equitable Pioneers' commenced business. . . .

Since that time two generations of 'doffers' [mill boys] have bought their butter and oatmeal at the . . . shop, and many a . . . wholesome meal, and many a warm jacket . . . which articles would never have reached their stomachs or their shoulders, had it not been for . . . the co-operative weavers.

. . . Charles Howarth proposed the plan of dividing profits . . . quarterly among the members in proportion to their purchases. . . .

At the end of the first quarter the Rochdale Society did pay a dividend of 3d [1½p] in the pound. The second dividend was 4d [2p] . . . the 7th 1s 2d [6p] . . . the 9th 1s 6d [8p]. . . . In 1844 the number of members was 28, amount of capital £28; in 1857, the number of members was 1,850, the amount of capital £15,142. . . ."

C **A Co-operative advertisement, taken from 'Handbook of the 27th Co-operative Congress', published in 1895.**

Questions

1 *Read Source* [A] .

a Why did the weavers meet together in 1843 and what did they resolve to do?

b By what means did they raise funds for the project?

c According to Source [A] how long did it take to plan and set up the Society?

d The nineteenth-century co-operative movement had two main features – the sale of goods and the manufacture of goods. How does Source [A] show that both features were present in the original objectives of the Rochdale Equitable Pioneers?

e Why do you think they were called 'Pioneers'?

f From the evidence in Source [A] give one *fact* and one *opinion* implied by the author.

g The phrase 'self-help' appears in the title of the book from which Source [A] is an extract. Can you explain, in your own words, what this phrase means?

h Describe, in not less than 100 words, the events of 1843–44 from the point of view of one of the weavers who formed the Rochdale Society. Include the following four pairs of words (in any order) in your answer: we thought; we believed; we feared; we hoped.

2 *Read Source* [B] .

a What evidence in Source [B] indicates that the co-operative store in Toad Lane started in a small way? Give more than one example.

b What benefits did the members get from the Rochdale Society, besides being able to purchase goods?

c In what ways did the co-operative store differ from the ordinary type of shop?

d Each quarter of the year a percentage of the profits was paid out to members. What was this payment called?

e What evidence suggests that the retail store for food and clothing was the most successful achievement of the Rochdale Pioneers?

f After the payment of the dividends, the number of members of the co-operative rose rapidly. Can you suggest why?

3 *Look at Source* [C] .

a Source [C] is an advertisement. Is it concerned with: (i) a co-operative village; (ii) a co-operative shop; or (iii) a co-operative factory?

b What was manufactured in the Woodhouse Mills, Huddersfield?

c What evidence suggests that the Mills had a good reputation for their products?

d How were the profits of co-operative production at Woodhouse Mills divided?

Linking evidence

4 There were various earlier unsuccessful efforts to set up co-operative societies. Using Sources [A] and [B] can you suggest why the Rochdale Pioneers succeeded after others had failed?

5 Which Source [A] – [C] would you consider to be the *most* reliable in terms of providing *facts*?

6 What were the main differences between the Rochdale Co-operative (Sources [A] and [B]) and the Woodhouse Mills Co-operative (Source [C])?

7 Is the co-operative movement still in existence? Can you give an example?

22 The Great Exhibition

A **Extract from a speech given by Prince Albert in London in 1849.**

". . . Gentlemen . . . we are living at a period of most wonderful transition. . . . the . . . division of labour . . . is being extended to all branches of science, industry, and art . . . no sooner is a discovery or invention made, than it is already improved upon and surpassed by competing efforts; the products of all quarters of the globe are placed at our disposal. . . .

So man . . . has . . . to conquer Nature to his use . . . Science discovers these laws of power, motion, and transformation; industry applies them . . . art teaches us the . . . laws of beauty and symmetry. . . .

Gentlemen – The Exhibition of 1851 is to give us a true test and a living picture of the point of development at which the whole of mankind has arrived . . . and a new starting point from which all nations will be able to direct their further exertions. . . ."

B **Description of the opening of the Great Exhibition on 1 May 1851, from the 'Life and Letters of Lord Macaulay'.**

"A fine day for the opening . . . I was struck by the number of foreigners in the streets. . . . there must have been near three hundred thousand people in Hyde Park. . . . The boats . . . darting across the lake; the flags; the music; the guns; – everything was exhilarating. . . ."

C **Extract from 'The Adventures of Mr and Mrs Sandboys, and Family', by Henry Mayhew, published in 1851.**

"The shilling folk may be an 'inferior' class of visitors, but at least, they know something about the works of industry, and what they do not know, they have come to learn. . . . Here you see a railway guard . . . hurrying, with his family, towards the locomotive department . . . among the agricultural implements, saunter clusters of countrymen in smockfrocks. . . .

But the chief centres of curiosity are the power-looms, and in front of these are gathered small groups of artisans [craftsmen], and labourers, and young men whose coarse red hands tell you they do something for their living. . . .

Round the electro-plating and the model diving-bell are crowds jostling one another for a foremost place. At the steam brewery, crowds of men and women are . . . ascending and descending the stairs; youths are watching the model carriages moving along the new pneumatic railway; young girls are waiting to see the hemispherical lamp-shades made out of a flat sheet of paper; whether it be the noisy flax-crushing machine . . . or the clatter of the Jacquard lace machine . . . round each . . . are anxious, intelligent . . . artisans, and farmers, and servants, and youths, and children clustered. . . ."

D **A cartoon from 'Punch', 1851.**

THE POUND AND THE SHILLING.
"Whoever Thought of Meeting You Here?"

Questions

1 *Read Source* A .
   a According to Prince Albert, what was the purpose of the Exhibition?
   b Explain the connection Prince Albert was making between 'Science', 'Industry' and 'Art'.

2 *Read Source* B .
   a When was the Great Exhibition opened?
   b In which London Park was the Exhibition held?
   c What evidence indicates that the Exhibition was well attended and a great success?
   d Does Source B *by itself, prove* that the Exhibition was a great success? Explain your answer.

3 *Read Source* C .
   a Admission into the Exhibition was 2s 6d (12½p) on Fridays, 5s (25p) on Saturdays, and one shilling (5p) from Mondays to Thursdays. Explain why some visitors were described as 'shilling folk' and why they might be regarded as an inferior class of people.
   b Give some examples of 'shilling folk'. Why does Mayhew approve of them?
   c Mayhew believed that some wealthy visitors came to the Great Exhibition 'to be seen rather than to see'. Explain what he meant.

4 *Look at Source* D .
   a This *Punch* cartoon is entitled 'The Pound and the Shilling'. Which group (left or right) is meant to represent 'the pound' and which group (left or right) 'the shilling'?
   b Describe each of the two groups, and list the differences between them.
   c What is the cartoonist trying to say about the Great Exhibition:
   (i) that people were surprised to meet old friends there; (ii) that people of all social classes attended the Exhibition; or (iii) that the Exhibition was intended only for the upper class?
   d What can you tell from the cartoon about the social class of: (i) the 'pound' folk; (ii) the 'shilling' folk?
   e The cartoonist has included one line of an *imaginary* conversation between the two groups: 'Whoever thought of meeting you here?' Continue the conversation between the two groups to show what they thought of their visit.

Linking evidence

5 What does the length of time between Prince Albert's speech (Source A) and the opening of the Exhibition (Source B) indicate about the preparations and the scale of the planned event?

6 Why would it be useful for an historian to have more than one type of source recording the same event?

7 Does the appearance of the 'shilling people' in the cartoon (Source D) match the description of the 'shilling folk' described in Source C ? Give reasons for your answer.

8 What evidence in Sources A – D could be used to support the view that the Great Exhibition united all classes of people in pride for their nation?

9 Write a letter describing 'your day at the Great Exhibition' to a member of your family who has recently emigrated to the United States.

23 Numbering the people

A A cartoon by George Cruikshank which shows the problems experienced by the 1851 census enumerators (counters).

B A census enumerator (counter) interviewing occupants of a lodging-house in Gray's Inn Lane, London, in 1871.

C Extract from the 'Census Report' of 1863.

"TOWNS AND CITIES

The English nation . . . has assumed the character of a preponderating city population [this means 'most people live in cities'] . . . rapidly as the population has increased, it has not kept pace with the progress of industry and wealth. . . . The rates of increase varied to a great extent; thus Birkenhead . . . had 667 inhabitants at the beginning of the century, and 51,649 in 1861. Canterbury had at the same dates 9,000 and 21,324 . . . York grew from 16,846 to 40,433 . . . Bradford from 13,264 to 106,218. In population, next to London stands Liverpool (443,938), and Manchester (357,979) . . . Birmingham (296,076) . . . Leeds (207,165), and Sheffield (185,172) . . . Bristol (154,093). In the vicinity of these large cities, and beyond their boundaries, are often towns and populous districts which are in constant relation with them . . . London still maintains its pre-eminence as the metropolis of the empire . . . population was 958,863 in 1801, and 2,803,989 in 1861. . . ."

Questions

1 *Look at Sources* **A** *and* **B** .
   a The Sources are different in their *form*. Source **A** is a cartoon. What is Source **B** ?
   b What event is taking place and in what year in: (i) Source **A** ; (ii) Source **B** ? What period of time separates the two Sources?
   c How do you know which figure is the enumerator in both Sources **A** and **B** ?
   d In Source **A** the cartoonist is drawing attention to the problems of taking an accurate census. What are they?
   e Do you think that the cartoonist (Source **A**) has exaggerated the difficulties in taking the census? Does the enumerator in Source **B** face similar problems?
   f Is there any difference in the kinds of people being counted in Sources **A** and **B** ? Detail the differences in a short paragraph.

2 *Read Source* **C** .
   a When was the Report written and on which two censuses is it based?
   b Is the extract from the 1863 Report concerned mainly with: (i) urban population growth; (ii) rural population decline; or (iii) national trends in population migration?
   c Which towns and cities showed the greatest rate of increase during the period? Can you suggest why?
   d What evidence in Source **C** indicates that the total population of the nation had increased rapidly in the first half of the nineteenth century?
   e The Report considers the changes which had taken place over a period of: (i) 25 years; (ii) 60 years; or (iii) 75 years?
   f Was the first official national census of population taken in: (i) 1801; (ii) 1861; or (iii) 1901?

Linking evidence

3 Which of the Sources **A** – **C** do you consider would be: (i) of *most* use to an historian; and (ii) of *least* use to an historian? Explain why.

4 A census is still taken in Britain every ten years.
   a Do you know by what method a census is taken at the present time?
   b Do you think people should be forced to fill in the census form? Give reasons for your answer.
   c Which people might find the information gathered in the census useful, and why?
   d Which kinds of people might not want to be included in the census? Can you suggest why?

24 Emigration

A A cartoon from 'Punch'.

HERE   AND   THERE;
OR, EMIGRATION A REMEDY.

B **Extract from the 'Colonial Land and Emigration Commission Annual', 1848.**
"*RULES*
1 Every passenger to rise at 7 a.m. . . .
2 Breakfast from 8–9 a.m., dinner at 1 p.m., supper at 6 p.m.
3 Passengers to be in their beds by 10 p.m.
4 No naked light to be allowed.
5 The passengers when dressed, to roll up their beds, to sweep the decks, including the space under the bottom of berths, and to throw the dirt overboard. . . .
6 . . . sweepers . . . to clean the ladders, hospitals, and . . . to sweep the decks after every meal. . . .
7 Two days in the week to be applied by the Master as washing days. . . .
8 The . . . cooking vessels to be cleaned every day. . . .
9 Hospitals to be established . . . in ships carrying 100 passengers. . . .
10 No spirits or gunpowder to be taken on board by any passenger.
11 No smoking allowed between decks.

C **Extract from 'Old Skibbereen', a traditional Irish ballad.**
"Oh, father dear I oft times hear you speak of Erin's Isle [Ireland]
Her lofty scenes her valleys green, her mountains wild and high
They say it is a lovely land where-in a prince might dwell
Oh, why did you abandon it the reason to me tell.

★　　★　　★

Oh son I loved my native land with energy and pride
Till a blight came o'er my crops – my sheep, my cattle died
My rent and taxes were too high, I could not them redeem
And that's the cruel reason that I left old Skibbereen

★　　★　　★

Oh well do I remember the bleak December day
The landlord and the sheriff came to drive us all away
They set my roof on fire with their cursed English spleen [spite]
And that's another reason I left old Skibbereen."

D The destinations and numbers of emigrants from the United Kingdom in the years 1821, 1831, 1841 and 1851.

	Canada	USA	Australia and New Zealand	Elsewhere
1821	12,995	4,958	320	384
1831	58,067	23,418	1,561	114
1841	38,164	45,017	32,625	2,786
1851	42,605	267,357	21,532	4,472

Questions

1 *Look at Source* A .
  a The cartoon comments on emigration. What are 'Here' and 'There' meant to represent?
  b List all the ways in which the cartoonist has illustrated the differences between the two families.
  c Do you think that the cartoon: (i) portrays an accurate picture of emigration; (ii) gives a misleading impression; or (iii) is too simplistic? Say why.
  d Source A is clearly biased in favour of emigration. Does that mean that it is of no use to an historian studying the subject?
  e If you had been a member of the family shown 'Here', would you have wanted to emigrate or not? Write a short paragraph to explain your choice.
  f From the evidence in Source A , give one *cause* and one *result* of emigration.

2 *Read Source* B .
  a Source B is a list of rules in operation on board an emigrant ship. Can you suggest why it was necessary to have so many strict rules?
  b Would the evidence in Source B be sufficient, *by itself*, to make a study of life on board an emigrant ship? Give reasons for your answer.
  c What attempts were made to prevent the spread of sickness on board an emigrant ship?

3 *Read Source* C .
  a What is Source C ?
  b What memories did the father have of his native land? Had he wanted to leave Ireland?
  c List all the reasons why the father had to emigrate.
  d Many emigrants suffered from 'home-sickness' and a longing for their native land. Is there any evidence in Source C which might support this?

4 *Look at Source* D .
  a Which country received the highest number of emigrants from the UK in 1821 and 1831?
  b Which country received a greatly increased number of emigrants in 1851?
  c Which countries received the least numbers of emigrants in each of the four years shown (excluding 'Elsewhere')?
  d Describe how the pattern of emigration changed between 1821 and 1851.
  e What problems would an historian face in trying to establish patterns of emigration from figures taken at only ten-year intervals?

Linking evidence

5 Over four million people emigrated from the UK between 1815 and 1851. Why might the Government and the local rate-payers have favoured emigration for the poor and unemployed?

6 Can you suggest reasons why emigration to the USA and Canada was more popular than emigration to Australia and New Zealand?

25 A new model town

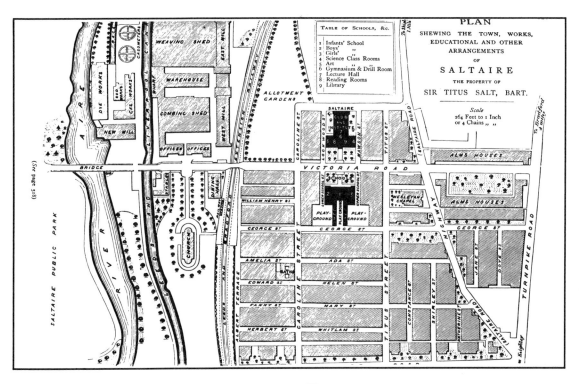

A The town of Saltaire.

B The motives of Sir Titus Salt.
"I thought that by concentrating my works within one locality I might provide occupation for my sons. . . . I also hope to do good to my fellow men."

C A notice at the entrance to the town of Saltaire.
"Abandon beer all ye who enter here."

D An artist's view of the town of Saltaire.

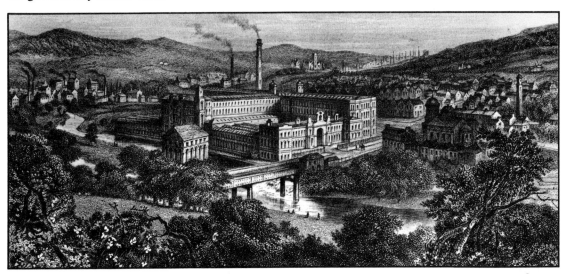

Questions

1 *Look at Source* A .
  a Would you describe Source A as: (i) a map; (ii) an aerial photograph; or (iii) a plan?
  b Who owned the town, and on which river was it sited? Can you suggest why it was called Saltaire?
  c Source A shows that the works were situated on the Leeds and Liverpool Canal. What evidence can you find that the Canal was used for transport?
  d What other forms of transport passed through the town?
  e What advantages were there for both the works and the town's inhabitants from the transport facilities?
  f Can you suggest which two forms of power were used in Saltaire?
  g Why were the dye works sited close to the River Aire?
  h What was produced at the works? What evidence indicates that a number of processes were carried out?
  i What does the large number of streets indicate about the size of the workforce at Saltaire?
  j What provision was made for education in Saltaire?
  k What evidence is there that the inhabitants could grow some of their own food?
  l What evidence is there that Salt had concern for his workers outside factory hours?

2 *Read Source* B .
  a What were Titus Salt's motives in building the new town of Saltaire?
  b Is Titus Salt stating *facts* or expressing *opinions*? Explain your answer.

3 *Read Source* C .
  a Why do you think this notice was put up?
  b Why do you think that Salt and many others did not approve of alcohol?

Linking evidence

4 Saltaire had no police station and no pawn shop. What does this suggest about the community?

5 Which other amenity is absent from the town which might be one reason why a police station and pawn shop were unnecessary?

6 Comparing all the Sources, which do you think would be of most use to an historian? Give reasons for your choice.

7 Can you suggest some of the benefits, and drawbacks, of living and working in Saltaire?

8 Using the word 'model' in the sense that it means something worthy of imitation, why do you think Saltaire was referred to as a model town?

26 The 1870 Education Act

A Extract from a speech by the Liberal MP, W. E. Forster, in 1870.

". . . We must not delay. Upon the speedy provision of elementary education depends our industrial prosperity. . . It is no use trying to give technical teaching to our workforce without elementary education . . . if we leave our workforce any longer unskilled . . . they will become overmatched by the competition of the world. . . ."

B Extract from a speech by the Liberal MP, W. E. Forster, in 1870.

"Our object is to complete the present voluntary system, to fill the gaps sparing the public money where it can be done without. . . . We see that a district must be supplied . . . we therefore say it must be supplied by means of rates, aided by money voted by Parliament. . . . The School Boards are to provide the education."

C Cartoon from 'Punch', 2 July 1870.

D Extracts from the 1870 (Forster) Education Act.

". . . Where . . . there is an insufficient amount of . . . school accommodation for any school district, a school board shall be formed . . . and shall supply such deficiency.

. . . [there shall be] instruction in religious subjects . . . and any scholar may be withdrawn by his parent . . . school shall be open at all times to the inspection of any of Her Majesty's inspectors. . . .

Every child attending a school provided by any school board shall pay such weekly fee as may be prescribed, but the school board may remit [pay] the whole or any part of such fee in the case of any child when . . . the parent of such child is unable from poverty to pay the same.

Every school board . . . may make byelaws . . . requiring the parents of children . . . not less than five years nor more than thirteen years . . . to cause such children (unless there is some reasonable excuse) to attend school . . . determining the time during which children are so to attend school. . . ."

"OBSTRUCTIVES."

Mr. Punch (to Bull A I). "YES, IT'S ALL VERY WELL TO SAY, 'GO TO SCHOOL!' HOW ARE THEY TO GO TO SCHOOL WITH THOSE PEOPLE QUARRELLING IN THE DOORWAY? WHY DON'T YOU MAKE 'EM 'MOVE ON'?"

Questions

1 *Read Source* [A] .
   a Why did W. E. Forster believe it was necessary to provide elementary education for all?
   b Elementary education was largely concerned with reading, writing and arithmetic. Can you explain the connection between elementary education and 'technical teaching'?
   c Did Forster believe that the provision of elementary education was urgent or not? Quote two phrases from the extract to support your answer.

2 *Read Source* [B] .
   a Is the subject of Source [B] : (i) the voluntary system of raising public money; (ii) increasing the rates; or (iii) ways of providing education for all children?
   b Before 1870, had elementary education for poor children been provided by: (i) Parliament; (ii) School Boards; or (iii) voluntary organizations?
   c Why might there be 'gaps' in 'the present voluntary system'?
   d How did W. E. Forster intend to provide education to fill the gaps in the voluntary system?

3 *Look at Source* [C] .
   a What is the setting for the cartoon?
   b How does the cartoonist show that the children are prepared to go to school? Which book is the young boy carrying?
   c What is Mr Punch saying to the policeman? (The policeman represents John Bull, the symbol of public opinion.)
   d Public opinion wanted education for all children. In what ways are the children being prevented from going to school?
   e The cartoonist is showing some of the difficulties in providing schools paid for out of rates and taxes. Are the people quarrelling in the school doorway: (i) civil servants; (ii) clergymen; or (iii) schoolteachers? Give reasons for your answer.
   f In not less than 30 words explain what the cartoonist is trying to say about the 'obstructions' to extending education to all children.

4 *Read Source* [D] .
   a Would school boards be set up in every school district in the country? Explain your answer.
   b Did all children have to pay fees to attend school? Explain your answer.
   c Under the terms of the 1870 Education Act were all children *compelled* to attend school?
   d The Education Act refers to 'instruction in religious subjects'. Why might this phrase cause arguments between different Churches and lead to some Churches opposing the introduction of elementary education?

Linking evidence

5 Was the author of Sources [A] and [B] involved in the passing of the 1870 Education Act? What is his point of view?

6 Sources [A] and [B] are from a speech made in Parliament. Source [C] is a cartoon. Does this mean that Source [C] is of less use to an historian than Sources [A] and [B] in studying this subject? Give reasons for your answer.

7 Does Source [C] support or contradict Sources [A] and [B] ? Explain your answer.

8 Did the 1870 Education Act (Source [D]) solve any of the problems outlined in Sources [A] and [B] ? Give reasons for your answer.

27 School attendance

A An artist's view of a School Board 'capture' from the 'Illustrated London News', 9 September 1871.

B Extract from an article in the 'Illustrated London News', 9 September 1871.

"The Elementary Education Act, contains some new provisions for compelling the attendance at school of children . . . if the Local School Boards wish . . . the community suffers a huge amount of mischief . . . from the idleness and ignorance, so common among the poor neglected youth of our towns. . . . The . . . London School Board, which is likely to set an example to other educational authorities throughout England and Wales, have already been extended to the catching of homeless boys . . . the officer employed by the Board . . . is experienced with the haunts and habits of these unhappy children . . . and has been accustomed now and then to seek them, with a police constable to aid him, at a very early hour of the morning. . . . They are inclined to hide in railway arches or underneath bridges, or in the sheds of building-yards, or in the cellars of unfinished houses. . . ."

C Extract from a Report from the Truants' School to members of Sheffield School Board.

"*SHEFFIELD SCHOOL BOARD: TRUANTS' SCHOOL AND FARM*
. . . In . . . 1877, the Board, with the view of securing better attendance at the Elementary Schools in the Borough, thought it desirable to establish a Truant School . . . for 4 years we have had continually over 80 boys, and . . . not a single death has occurred . . . the general health and physique of the boys very much improves during their period of detention. . . .

It frequently happens that boys who are committed by the magistrates to the Truants' School, have been very much more sinned against than sinning, and that their home surroundings have more to do or are very much more responsible for their falling into our hands than any misconduct on the part of the boys themselves; and past experience has shown us that there are numbers of those boys, which to license out to their own parents would simply be to make sure of their shortly being either sent back again, or committed to prison for some petty offence; and that this Farm work has enabled us to give training to these boys, which has readily secured situations for them, in which they are in a great measure free from such temptations, and have a fair chance of making good citizens."

Questions

1 *Look at Sources* Ⓐ *and* Ⓑ .

a What source of information could the artist have used in order to draw the picture (Source Ⓐ)?

b Write down *four* words or phrases in Source Ⓑ which you feel best describe the boys shown in the illustration (Source Ⓐ).

c Who is the man on the right in the illustration and what is he doing? Who is helping him in his task?

d Do you think the boys shown in the illustration would benefit in any way from an elementary education?

e Do you think the artist is sympathetic to the homeless boys, or not? Say why.

f 'The Education Act of 1870 made education compulsory for all children of elementary school age.' Is this statement *true* or *false*?

g In what ways did the London School Board try to deal with poor attendance at school?

h Why was the action taken by the London School Board regarded as being very important?

i Would you describe Source Ⓑ as a *biased* or *balanced* piece of evidence? Give reasons for your answer.

j How do you think the children in Sources Ⓐ and Ⓑ would feel about being compelled to attend school?

k In what ways does Source Ⓑ provide more information than Source Ⓐ ?

2 *Read Source* Ⓒ .

a Why did the Sheffield School Board establish a Truant School in 1877?

b Did the Report (Source Ⓒ) place most of the blame for truancy on: (i) the boys themselves; or (ii) their circumstances and surroundings? Quote evidence from the Report to support your answer.

c List all the ways in which the boys might benefit from attending a Truant School.

d Would you describe the Report (Source Ⓒ) as expressing mainly *fact* or *opinion*?

Linking evidence

3 Source Ⓐ is an illustration. Source Ⓒ is from an official School Report. Would Source Ⓐ be less useful than Source Ⓒ to an historian trying to find out about education and truancy?

4 'The main problem facing School Boards after the 1870 Education Act was low attendance.' How far does the evidence in Sources Ⓐ – Ⓒ support this statement?

5 Using evidence from Sources Ⓐ – Ⓒ , show how enforcing school attendance might improve the opportunities of poor children in obtaining regular work.

6 From the evidence in Sources Ⓐ – Ⓒ , can you say which groups of children were intended to be helped by the 1870 Education Act and the attempts to improve school attendance?

7 Many parents and children were bitterly opposed to compulsory education. There were many reasons for this. Can you suggest some of the reasons?

8 How does your school attempt to deal with problems of truancy today?

28   The Sheffield Outrages

A An artist's view of a sawgrinder at work in Sheffield in 1866.

B Adaptation of an extract from the examination of William Broadhead and others in 1867 after the Sheffield Outrages, quoted in 'The Sheffield Outrages', published in 1971.

"*Chairman* On 8 October 1866 Thomas Fearnehough's house was blown up?
Broadhead Yes.
Chairman Who caused that to be done?
Broadhead Me.
Chairman Whom did you employ?
Broadhead [Samuel] Crooks . . . Copley was with him.
Chairman Copley is a member of the Union I believe as well as Crooks?
Broadhead Yes.
Chairman How much did you give to Crooks for doing that?
Broadhead I think it was £15.

Evidence of Samuel Crooks
Chairman Did you blow up Fearnehough?
Crooks Yes, I am sorry to say that I did.
Chairman Who employed you to do that?
Crooks Broadhead.
Chairman Had you any quarrel at all with Fearnehough?
Crooks No.
Chairman Was it merely because you were set on by Broadhead that you blew him up?
Crooks Yes.
Chairman Did he tell you why he wanted Fearnehough blown up?
Crooks Yes, he was doing us a deal of injury . . . doing wrong in some way according to the rules . . . of the trade."

C Extract on the practice of 'rattening' during the Sheffield Outrages, from the 'First Report of the Trades Union Commission', published in 1867.

"*Robert Applegarth* . . . the rattening that we have heard of . . . in . . . the Sheffield trades is common to every trade, and what is meant by rattening is that if a man renders himself objectionable to those he is working with they try to make it unpleasant . . . to 'Put the man in Coventry' . . . is the mildest form of rattening. . . . Again, it is the practice in many trades to remove a man's working tools, not to steal them. Now, that is a thing which I do not . . . believe in at all, and it is . . . fast dying out. . . .

Mr Roebuck. You spoke of rattening, and made use of the mild phrase of 'removing' not 'stealing' tools. Now removing tools from a man I suppose takes away his power of doing his work . . . therefore deprives him of his wages . . . therefore reduces him to starvation?

Robert Applegarth . . . My society does not officially recognize the practice. . . . They discourage it."

D **Extract from 'Annals of Our Time' by Joseph Irving, published in 1869.**
"15 October 1866. Attempt . . . by agents of the Sawgrinders' Union in Sheffield to kill or maim one Fearnehough, who had withdrawn from their society. His house was blown up with gunpowder, but the inmates escaped with trifling injuries. The masters offered £1,000 reward . . . and the Government £100, for such information as would lead to a discovery of the perpetrators. . . ."

Questions

1 *Look at Source* **A** .
  a What type of source is Source **A** ?
  b Describe what is happening in the picture.
  c In what ways might accidents and injuries at work occur?
  d Why might it be useful for the worker shown in Source **A** to belong to a trade union?
  e How useful would this Source be for purposes of historical inquiry?

2 *Read Source* **B** .
  a Why were William Broadhead and Samuel Crooks being examined?
  b What did Broadhead and Crooks admit to?
  c In what ways was Broadhead's part in the outrage different from that of Crooks?
  d Were all those involved in the incident trade union members?

3 *Read Source* **C** .
  a From the evidence in Source **C** , can you give an explanation of the practice of 'rattening'?
  b Was the practice of rattening found only in the Sheffield trades?
  c Why did taking a man's working tools reduce him to starvation?
  d Robert Applegarth was General Secretary of the Amalgamated Society of Carpenters and Joiners. Was his trade union in favour of rattening? Explain your answer.

4 *Read Source* **D** .
  a Is Source **D** a primary or a secondary source? How do you know?
  b What happened on 15 October 1866?
  c According to Source **D** , why was the Sawgrinders' Union angry with Fearnehough?
  d Suggest why the masters (the owners of the works) were prepared to offer a large sum of money as a reward. Give more than one reason if you can.

Linking evidence

5 Why do you think the events in Sheffield in 1866 were described as 'Outrages'? Who do you think would be 'outraged' by the events?

6 How might such 'outrages' and practices affect the attitude of the public towards trade unions?

7 Do the Sources **A** – **D** provide enough evidence to assess the actions of the Sawgrinders' Union in Sheffield? What questions would you or an historian be likely to ask before making a judgement? Where might you find the evidence which would provide some answers?

8 In what ways might the evidence in Sources **B** – **D** be used by masters and politicians wanting to reform or to limit the powers of trade unions? Explain your answer.

9 If you were Robert Applegarth how would you argue the case for trade unions? Refer to the information in Sources **A** – **D** in your answer.

29 Looking for work

A An artist's view of the registration of unemployed at Chelsea, London, in 1887, from the 'Illustrated London News'.

B One of the earliest Labour Exchanges, in Camberwell, London in 1910.

C Extract from 'From Workhouse to Westminster: The Life Story of Will Crooks', by G. Haw, published in 1907.
"I went down to the riverside at Shadwell. No work was to be had there. Then I called at another place in Limehouse. No hands wanted. So I looked in at home and got two slices of bread in paper and walked eight miles [13 km] to a cooper's yard in Tottenham. All in vain. I dragged myself back to Clerkenwell. Still no luck . . . turned towards home in despair. By the time I reached Stepney I was dead beat . . . called at a friend's in Commercial Road for a little rest. They gave me some Irish stew and twopence [1p] to ride home. I managed to walk home and gave the twopence to my wife. . . ."

D Extract from 'From Workhouse to Westminster: The Life Story of Will Crooks' by G. Haw, published in 1907.
"A man who is out of work for long nearly always degenerates [loses self-respect] . . . if a decent fellow falls out in October and fails to get a job by say March he loses his anxiety to work. The exposure, the insufficient food, his half-starved condition have such a deteriorating effect upon him that he becomes indifferent whether he gets work or not. He thus passes from the unemployed state to the unemployable state. It ought to be the duty of the nation to see that a man does not become degenerate."

Questions

1 *Compare Sources* [A] *and* [B] .
   a The two illustrations are different in *form*. Source [A] is a drawing. What is Source [B] ?
   b Which type of source, in your opinion, is likely to be of most use to an historian?
   c List all the similarities and differences between the two illustrations. How do you account for these?
   d What do you notice about the people *looking* for work in both Sources [A] and [B] ?
   e Both Sources ([A] and [B]) show attempts to find work for the unemployed.
      (i) Which Source, [A] or [B] , shows that being run on a voluntary basis?
      (ii) Which Source, [A] or [B] , shows that being organized on an official basis?

2 *Read Source* [C] .
   a Which places did the author of the extract (Source [C]) visit to look for work? Was he successful?
   b Why did he walk home when he had been given 'twopence to ride home'?

3 *Read Source* [D] .
   a Explain the difference between 'unemployed state' and 'unemployable state'.
   b From the evidence, give one *fact* and one *opinion* implied by the author of Source [D] .

Linking evidence

4 The Liberal Government set up Labour Exchanges in 1909. Which of the Sources shows a Labour Exchange at work? What was its purpose?

5 The voluntary worker in Source [A] is shown writing down information. What sort of information do you think she would require from someone looking for work?

6 The same author wrote Sources [C] and [D] . Which of the Sources, [C] or [D] , records his own personal experiences? Which Source, [C] or [D] , gives his views of the effects of unemployment?

7 Using the following information write a conversation between the two men (standing in front of the desk) in Source [A] .

Persons in Source [A]	Period out of work	Words included in conversation	Evidence
1st man Age 58	6 months	I fear I think I believe	Sources [A] ,[C] ,[D]
2nd man Age 22	3 weeks	I hope I feel I expect	Sources [A] ,[C] ,[D]

From your reconstructed conversation suggest why the two men, living at the same time, thought and felt so differently.

30.1 Poverty and the Rowntree Report

BUDGET No. 5

LABOURER. WAGES 20s. [£1]

This family consists of five persons, a father, aged 49, mother, 47, and three daughters, age respectively 22, 13, 8. The mother "has a bad leg," and the eldest daughter is not strong enough to go out to work, as she is "suffering from weakness," which takes the form of rheumatism. The two younger children are at school. The house is clean and comfortable, the wife being an excellent manager. This budget was kept for eight consecutive weeks during May and June 1900. The total income during this period was £8. . . .

There is a deficiency of 40 per cent in the protein of this family's diet, and a deficiency of 41 per cent in its fuel value.

MENU OF MEALS PROVIDED DURING WEEK ENDING JUNE 23, 1900

	Breakfast.	Dinner.	Tea.	Supper.
Friday	Bread, butter, and tea.	Bacon, potatoes, and rhubarb pie.	Bread, butter, lettuce, and tea.	Bread, brawn, and coffee.
Saturday	Fried bacon, bread, tea.	Fish and potatoes.	Bread, butter, and tea.	Bread and cheese.
Sunday	Fried bacon, bread, tea.	Stewed rabbit, potatoes, cabbage, Yorkshire pudding.	Bread, butter, sweet cake, lettuce, tea.	Bread and cheese.
Monday	Fried bacon, bread, tea.	Rabbit, potatoes, rhubarb pie.	Bread, butter, sweet cake, tea.	Rhubarb pie.
Tuesday	Fried bacon, bread, tea.	Roast pork, potatoes, Yorkshire pudding.	Bread, butter, tea.	Rhubarb pie.
Wednesday	Fried bacon, bread, tea.	Cold pork, potatoes.	Bread, butter, tea.	Bread, cheese, and coffee.
Thursday	Bread, butter, tea.	Cold pork, potatoes, suet pudding.	Bread, butter, sweet cake, tea.	Brawn, bread, and coffee.

STATEMENT OF INCOME AND EXPENDITURE FOR EIGHT WEEKS

INCOME—

Wages, eight weeks at £1			£8 0 0
EXPENDITURE			
Food	.	.£4 7 0½	
Rent and rates	.	. 1 5 4	
Coal at 24s. ton	.	. 0 13 7	
Gas (1d. in slot meter)	.		0 2 0
Soap	.	. 0 2 0	
Sundries	.	. 0 1 7½	
Sick Club	.	. 0 4 0	
Life Insurance	.	. 0 1 8	
Clothing Club	.	. 0 2 0	
Kept by husband	.	. 0 16 0	
Surplus	.	. 0 4 9	
			£8 0 0

PURCHASES DURING JUNE 23, 1900

Friday.—1½ st. flour, 2s.; 1 st. potatoes, 8d.; ½ lb. lard, 3d.; 1 bag of coal, 1s. 6d.; 4 lbs. sugar, 6d.; ¼ lb. tea,, 6d.; 2 oz. coffee, 2d.; ¼ lb. brawn, 1½d.

Saturday.—Greens, 2d. milk, 7d.; ½ lb. butter, 6d.; rhubarb, 2d.; sticks, 2d.; lettuce, 1d.; radishes, 1d.; 1 lb soap, 3d.; 2 lbs bacon, 1s 2d.; rabbit, 1s.; ½ lb. cheese, 4d.; eggs, 3d.; 1 mackerel, 4d.

Monday.—Insurance, 4d.; Sick Club, 6d.; Clothing Club, 3d.; gas, 3d.

Tuesday.—2½ lbs. pork, 1s. 6d.; onions, 1½d.

Wednesday.—¼ lb. suet, 2d.

Thursday.—¼ lb. brawn, 1½d.

(20s = 100p; 10s = 50p; 2s = 10p; 1s = 5p; 6d = 2½p)

A Extract from 'Poverty: A Study in Town Life' by Seebohm Rowntree, published in 1901.

B **Extract from 'Poverty: A Study of Town Life' by Seebohm Rowntree, published in 1901.**

"The life of a labourer is marked by five alternating periods of want and comparative plenty. During early childhood, unless his father is a skilled worker, he will probably be in poverty; this will last until he, or some of his brothers or sisters, begin to earn money and thus augment [add to] their father's wages sufficiently to raise the family above the poverty line [a level of income below which a family could not afford to buy food, shelter, fuel and clothing]. Then follows the period during which he is earning money and living under his parents' roof; for some portion of this period he will be earning more money than is required for lodging, food and clothes. This is his chance to save money. If he has saved enough to pay for furnishing a cottage, this period of prosperity may continue after marriage until he has two or three children, when poverty will again overtake him. This period of poverty will last perhaps for ten years, i.e., until the first child is fourteen years old and begins to earn wages; but if there are more than three children it may last longer. While the children are earning, and before they leave the home to marry, the man enjoys another period of prosperity – possibly, however, only to sink back again into poverty when his children have married and left him, and he himself is too old to work, for his income has never permitted his saving enough for him and his wife to live upon for more than a short time."

Questions

1 *Read Source* A .
  a How many persons did the family consist of?
  b On whose wages did the family solely depend?
  c How much did the labourer earn *each week*?
  d Why were other members of the family unable to contribute to the income?
  e What evidence can you find to indicate that the labourer received his wages on a Friday?
  f How do you know the family baked their own bread?
  g Suggest *two* reasons why bread and potatoes formed a major part of the week's menu.
  h Which 'greens' did the labourer's family purchase?
  i What had happened to the family menu by mid-week? Include evidence to support your answer, both from the menu and from the timing of purchases.
  j Which forms of fuel and energy were used in the house? Given the time of year (June) can you suggest what they were used for?
  k How much did the labourer's family pay each week into social clubs and life insurance?
  l How much money did the labourer keep for himself each week?
  m Given the details of the expenditure (*purchases*) of the labourer's family, what is *your opinion* on the sum of money kept each week by the husband?
  n How much money was left over or surplus at the end of *each week*?
  o Can you suggest any reasons why members of this family were often in poor health?
  p Do you think the labourer's family *necessarily* considered themselves to be poor?

2 *Read Source* B .
  a During which periods of his life did the labourer enjoy some prosperity? Explain why this was so.
  b Why might the labourer sink back into poverty again?
  c Was a labourer ever really free from the threat of poverty?
  d Is Source B mainly concerned with *fact* or with *opinion*?

30.2 Poverty and the Rowntree Report

BUDGET No. 24

(Three Adults and Three Children)

LIST OF FOOD STUFFS USED DURING WEEK ENDING MAY 24, 1901

1st. flour, 1s. 5d; 1½ lbs. self-raising flour, 3d.; 1 oz. yeast, 1d.; 1 lb. lard. 6d.; 2 lbs. jam, 9d.; 8 lbs. oatmeal, 7½d.; 2½ lbs. butter, 2s. 11d.; ½ pt. cream, 10d.; cream cheese, 5d.; ½ lb. tea, 1s.; 3 lbs. treacle, 9d.; 2 lbs. beef-steak, 2s.; 1 st. potatoes, 8d.; cauliflower, 4d.; rhubarb, 6d.; 8½ galls. milk, 3s. 6d.; ½ lb. marmalade, 2½d.; asparagus, 6d.; 1 lb. 2 oz. beefsteak, 1s. 1½d.; ½ lb. currants, 3d.; ½ pt. vinegar, 1d.; lettuce, 2d.; 4 lbs. sugar, 3d.; ½ lb. bacon, 3½d.; 3 lbs. apples, 1s. 6d.; 6 oranges, 6d.; 1 lb. nutes, 5d.; 4½ lbs. beef, 3s. 4½d.; 17 eggs, 1s.; ¼ lb. potted shrimps, 6d.; ½ lb. mutton, 4d.; 6 bananas, 6d.; 2 lbs. halibut, 1s. 1d.; 12 oz. rice, 2d.; 2 oz. cornflour, 1½d.; 4½ oz. Benger's food, 7½d.; ¼ lb. cocoa, 6d.

MENU OF MEALS PROVIDED DURING WEEK ENDING MAY 24, 1901

	Breakfast.	Dinner.	Tea.	Supper.
Friday	Porridge, eggs, bread, butter, toast, boiled milk, tea.	Beef-steak, potatoes, cauliflower, sponge pudding, stewed rhubarb, cream, dates.	Bread, butter, tea-cake, pastry, tea.	Bread, butter, tea cake, Benger's food, cocoa.
Saturday	Porridge, beef-steak, toast, bread, butter, hot milk, tea.	Minced beef, potatoes, cauliflower, rhubarb pie, cream, oranges.	Bread, butter, buns, tarts, pastry, tea.	Bread, butter, sweet-cake, cocoa.
Sunday	Bacon and fried steak, break, butter, toast, tea.	Roast beef, potatoes, asparagus, cornflour, stewed rhubarb, cream.	Bread, butter, tea-cakes, fruit-cake, queen-cakes, cream cheese, lettuce, tea.	Bread, butter, Benger's food, hot milk.
Monday	Porridge, eggs, bread, butter, toast, tea.	Beef, Scotch potatoes, salad, boiled bread pudding, oranges.	Steak, bread, butter, tea-cakes, buns, tea.	Bread, butter, Benger's food, cocoa.
Tuesday	Porridge, cream cheese, bread, butter, toast, marmalade, tea.	Cold beef, salad, potatoes, rice pudding, stewed rhubarb, apples, oranges.	Potted shrimps, eggs, bread, butter, fruit-cake, tea-cake, jam, tea.	Bread, butter, Benger's food, cocoa.
Wednesday	Bread and milk, potted shrimps, eggs, bread, butter, toast, tea.	Minced beef, potatoes, cauliflower, rhubarb pie, apples, bananas.	Bread, butter, toast, cream cheese, jam, fruit-cake, tea.	Tea-cake, buns, Benger's food, cocoa.
Thursday	Porridge, stewed mutton, toast, bread, butter, tea.	Halibut, potatoes, bread and butter, pudding, stewed rhubarb, bananas, apples.	Eggs, bread, butter, toast, jam, tea.	Rice-cake and buns, Benger's food, cocoa.

(20s = 100p; 10s = 50p; 2s = 10p; 1s = 5p; 6d = 2½p)

C **Extract from 'Poverty: A Study in Town Life' by Seebohm Rowntree, published in 1901.**

3 *Read Source* C .

  a How many people were in the family?

  b Did the *quality* of the meals vary greatly from day to day? What does this indicate about the family income?

  c What kinds of fresh fruit and vegetables were included in the weekly menu? How much was spent each week on these items?

Linking evidence

4 Which of the menus, Budget No. 5 of the labourer's family (Source A) or Budget No. 24 of the servant-keeping class (Source C) would you consider to be the more varied diet? Say why.

5 What, in particular, does the labourer's family diet (Source A) lack which is present in the diet of the servant-keeping class (Source C)?

6 'Poverty can only be understood in relation to wealth or plenty.' Do you agree with this statement and if so, how does the information in Source C help you to understand the standard of living of the labourer's family (Source A)?

7 Seebohm Rowntree conducted his famous survey into poverty in York in 1899. To what extent do the Sources A – C extracted from the Report provide evidence of poverty, and the reasons for it?

8 Sources A – C have been used to provide evidence of poverty. In what other ways might the information be useful to an historian?

9 From the information in this section do you think that Seebohm Rowntree was sympathetic to the condition of the poor or not? Quote from the Sources to support your answer.

10 Which of the Sources A , B or C would be most useful in *understanding* poverty. Give your reasons.

11 What changes occurred in the years before 1914 to try to protect the poorer working families in the United Kingdom? (See pages 88–89).

12 Which of these Sources would be most useful to a political party looking for propaganda about the evils of poverty? Explain your answer.

31 Liberal reforms

A **Extract from 'British Economic and Social History 1700–1982' by C. P. Hill, published in 1985 (Fifth edition).**

". . . two measures of the Liberals in this period were of quite special importance – Old Age Pensions and National Insurance. Old Age Pensions were introduced in 1908 . . . they provided 5s [25p] a week for old people over seventy whose income was under 10s [50p] per week. . . . National Insurance began in 1911, and was modelled on the scheme introduced in Germany some twenty-five years previously. A state-run insurance fund was created; to it employers contributed 3d [1p] a week and employees 4d [2p] by means of stamps placed on cards, and the state added 2d [1p]. From the fund workmen could, through their 'approved' Friendly Societies [societies whose members paid subscriptions which enabled them to receive benefits in times of sickness and/or unemployment], draw benefit in times of sickness and unemployment . . . at first the insurance against unemployment applied only to wage-earners in building, engineering, shipbuilding, iron-founding, and a small number of other occupations. There was much opposition to this National Health and Unemployment Insurance, both from doctors who disliked the scheme of 'panels' of patients, and from well-to-do people who disapproved of the whole idea of these new 'social services'. . . ."

B **Liberal Party poster, 1911.**

C **Cartoon from 'Punch', 24 July 1912.**

D **Extracts from the National Insurance Act of 1911, from 'Statutes of the Realm'.** "An Act to provide for insurance against loss of Health and for the Prevention and Cure of Sickness, for Insurance against Unemployment. . . .

Insured Persons . . . shall be entitled . . . to the benefits in respect of health insurance and prevention of sickness. . . .

. . . funds for providing the benefits . . . and . . . the expenses of administration of those benefits shall be derived . . . from contributions made by or in respect of the contributors by themselves, or their employers, and . . . from moneys provided by Parliament. . . ."

Questions

1 *Read Source* A .
   a Is Source A a primary or a secondary source? Explain why.
   b Which two measures of the Liberal Government did the author of Source A consider to be of special importance?
   c Which people opposed the National Health and Unemployment Insurance, and why?

2 *Look at Source* B .
   a Who might benefit from the National Health Insurance Bill?
   b Does the poster support or oppose the National Health Insurance Bill?
   c Who produced the poster and why might this evidence be regarded as biased?

3 *Look at Source* C .
   a What is overflowing from John Bull's basin or bowl? (John Bull represents the British public.)
   b Name the Chancellor of the Exchequer represented by the workhouse master in an apron.
   c Does John Bull (the British public) want *more* or *less* social legislation?
   d What 'good thing' is still to come out of the copper in the corner, and be served to John Bull?
   e What evidence does the cartoonist provide to suggest that John Bull was 'fed up'?
   f Do you think the cartoonist was *for* or *against* more social legislation for the British public?

4 *Read Source* D .
   a Source D is an extract from an Act of Parliament. What did the Act seek to do, and when did it become law?
   b What benefits were insured persons entitled to? (See also Source A .)

Linking evidence

5 The cartoon (Source C) is based on a well-known illustration by George Cruikshank in a popular nineteenth-century novel (see pages 50–51). Which novel is the cartoon based on?

6 List all the ways in which the cartoonist has changed the original drawing.

7 What 'good things' (Source C) had the British public been 'fed' since 1906 (Sources A – D)?

8 Source B is a party political poster, Source D is an extract from an Act of Parliament. Does this mean that Source B would be less useful than Source D to an historian?

9 If you had been living in the early twentieth century would you have welcomed the National Health Act or not? Give reasons for your answer.

32 Free trade or protection?

A **Extract from a speech by Joseph Chamberlain in May 1903.**

"For sixty years we have tried to promote free trade with other countries by opening our markets to them while they have responded by closing their markets to us. We have completely failed. Wherever a foreign country has raised a tariff [tax] our exports [goods sent abroad to be sold] there have gone down. On the other hand, foreigners send us more and more of their manufactures. We are now the dumping ground of the world.

Free trade causes unemployment and low wages. It hinders national prosperity and therefore social reform. The working classes, more than any, suffer from it. Let us abandon it in favour of commercial union with our Empire. . . ."

B **Extract from a speech by the Liberal leader, Henry Campbell-Bannerman, in 1904.**

"I believe that protection [taxes or tariffs on imported goods, i.e. goods brought in from abroad] is immoral . . . and is founded on the exploitation of the community in the interests of favoured groups. It is corrupt, a menace to freedom and progress, an outrage to the democratic principle. It will lead to monopolies [where one person (or company) has control over a particular trade or type of business] and the trampling down of the working class, wage cuts and unemployment."

C **Cartoon from 'Punch', 1903.**

Questions

1 *Read Source* A .

   a Source A is about free trade and tariff reform. (i) How long had free trade been in operation by 1903? (ii) How had free trade been expected to work? (iii) Why was Chamberlain opposed to the policy of 'free trade'?

   b According to Chamberlain, why had UK exports fallen and imports increased?

   c Chamberlain wanted to abandon the policy of free trade. What policy did he favour?

   d How would you expect a believer in free trade to feel about Chamberlain's speech? Explain.

2 *Read Source* B .

   a What evidence in Source B indicates that Campbell-Bannerman was opposed to protection?

   b Why did he believe that protection was immoral?

   c What did he believe would be the results of 'protection'?

3 *Look at Source* C .

   a Describe the figures in the cartoon which are meant to represent: (i) Joseph Chamberlain; (ii) Arthur Balfour.

   b Are they moving in the direction of free trade or in the direction of protectionism?

   c How does the cartoonist suggest that the Prime Minister, Arthur Balfour, could not move as fast as Joseph Chamberlain? What does this tell us about the attitude of: (i) Chamberlain; (ii) Balfour to the policy of protectionism?

   d In the top right-hand corner of the cartoon the artist has included a cartoon published in the 1840s, which shows a reluctant Prime Minister (Sir Robert Peel) being led in the direction of free trade. The title of Source C is 'History Reverses Itself'. Explain this title.

   e Do you think the cartoonist was: (i) biased in favour of free trade; (ii) biased in favour of protectionism; or (iii) making a fair comment? Explain your answer.

Linking evidence

4 Does Source B *support* or *oppose* the views expressed in Source A ?

5 Would you describe Sources A and B as statements of *fact* or *opinion*?

6 Sources A – C are from the same period of time, 1903–04. How do you explain such different attitudes being expressed at the same time in history?

7 For each of the following words write a sentence to show that you understand the meaning: (i) free trade; (ii) protectionism; (iii) tariff; (iv) trade; (v) exports; (vi) imports.

33.1 Women at war

A **Extract from 'Changing Horizons: Britain 1914–80' by W. O. Simpson, published in 1986.**

"One of the most striking features of the women's suffrage movement [the campaign for votes for women] was the zeal which some of its leaders showed for the war effort. The *Suffragette* was re-christened *Britannia*. Mrs Emmeline Pankhurst led a demonstration demanding 'The Right to Serve'. Her wishes were granted. Under the pressure of necessity women's employment went up rapidly. . . . The growth in anti-suffragist sentiment, clearly visible in 1914, was effectively reversed by the spectacle of women munitions [weapons of war] workers, bus conductresses, landgirls, police constables and nurses all making their contribution to the war effort. . . ."

B **First World War posters.**

C **Extracts from articles in 'The Times' about women on Glasgow's tramways.**

"Two women conductors are being employed, as an experiment, by the Glasgow Corporation Tramways Department. Nearly 2,000 men have left to join the Forces . . . and it has consequently been found difficult to maintain a full service. . . . (30 March 1915)

The employment of women as tramcar conductors has proved a complete success. In the first instance two women who had had several years' experience on the clerical staff of the Corporation Tramways Department were employed as an experiment. . . .

During the past week eight other women, none of whom had any previous experience of tramway work, have been engaged with equal success. . . . (19 April 1915)

The Tramways Committee of the Glasgow Corporation yesterday decided that, in addition to the eight already serving, other women should be engaged as tramway-car conductors to fill the vacancies, 300 or 400 in number. . . . (22 April 1915)"

Questions

1 *Read Source* A .
   a Is Source A a primary or a secondary source?
   b The women's suffrage movement pursued a militant campaign to obtain the vote for women. What event halted many of their activities?
   c What evidence in Source A indicates that the suffragettes supported the war effort?
   d By 1914 many people were against the suffragettes because of the actions they had taken in demanding the right to vote. Why did public opinion change after 1914?

2 *Look at Source* B .
   a What did the women shown in the two posters have in common?
   b For what purpose do you think these posters were produced? Explain your answer.
   c Which kinds of work were women being asked to do?
   d Using the evidence in the posters, describe the ways in which the artists have tried to make the occupations attractive to women.
   e Can you suggest why work on the land and in the munitions factories was so important during the war years?

3 *Read Source* C .
   a Why did the Glasgow Corporation Tramways Department begin to employ women as conductors on tramcars in 1915?
   b Why was the employment of women as conductors regarded as 'an experiment'?
   c What evidence indicates that the 'experiment' was a success?
   d What do the extracts suggest about the pre-war attitude to women being employed for this type of job?

33.2 Women at war

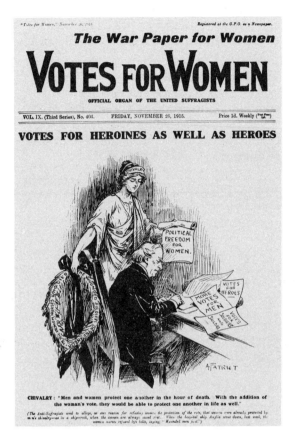

D The front cover of the 26 November 1915 edition of the magazine, 'Votes for Women'. The caption reads: 'The Anti-Suffragists used to allege, as one reason for refusing women the protection of the vote, that women were already protected by men's chivalry [polite behaviour] – as in a shipwreck, when the women are always saved first. When the hospital ship *Anglia* went down last week, the women nurses refused lifebelts, saying "wounded men first".'

E Extract from a speech by Lord Birkenhead in the House of Lords, May 1928.
". . . Had it not been for the War . . . we should have continued . . . to resist this measure for an indefinite period of time.

Let me describe to your Lordships, how . . . we descended the slippery slope. First of all it was not proposed that women should be included. Then a member of the House of Commons said that . . . it was quite impossible to exclude from the franchise [the right to vote] the brave men who had supported our cause in the field. That argument . . . was accepted . . . and accordingly the soldiers were admitted, subject to the qualification of age. Then another member of the House arose and said: 'If you are extending the franchise to our brave soldiers in recognition of their valour on the field how about our brave munition workers.' That argument too was difficult to resist. . . . Then an insidious [cunning] and subtle member of the House said, 'How about our brave women munition workers?' And having once on principle yielded to the first argument, it was absolutely impossible to resist the second."

4 *Look at Source* D .
  a What type of source is Source D ? When was it published and for what purpose?
  b 'Chivalry' is holding a wreath bearing the words 'To the women nurses who died. The wounded soldiers of the *Anglia*'. Explain the connection between the wreath and the caption to the illustration.
  c How did 'Chivalry' use the episode of the *Anglia* to argue for women's right to vote?
  d What is the seated man asking for?

5 *Read Source* E .
  a What was the 'measure' referred to in Source E ?
  b Was the author of Source E in favour of voting rights for women, or not? Quote words and phrases from the Source to support your answer.
  c Do you think the argument put forward in Source E to obtain the vote for women was an effective one or not? Give reasons for your answer.
  d Would you describe the evidence in Source E as mainly *fact* or *opinion*?
  e What evidence in Source E could be used to support the view that Lord Birkenhead was biased in his attitude concerning voting rights for women?

Linking evidence

6 In 1918 an Act of Parliament gave women over thirty years of age the right to vote. Was the contribution of women to the war effort: (i) the *only* reason; or (ii) the *main* reason for the Act being passed?

7 What evidence in Sources A – E indicates that the First World War gave many women the opportunity to undertake work which had previously been considered as only suitable for men?

8 What evidence in Sources A – E indicates that women were successful in filling jobs previously reserved for men?

9 From the evidence in Sources A – E what jobs were undertaken by women during the war years, 1914–18?

10 In what ways do Sources B and D support the argument used in Source E ?

11 Using Sources A – D write a letter to Lord Birkenhead (Source E) explaining to him the reasons why women should have the right to vote.

12 Give two results of the First World War which contributed to the changing role of women.

13 Sources A – D indicate some of the tasks undertaken by women during the First World War. Knowing how important their contribution to the war effort was, how do you think they might feel about not being able to vote in General Elections?

34 Unemployment in the inter-war years

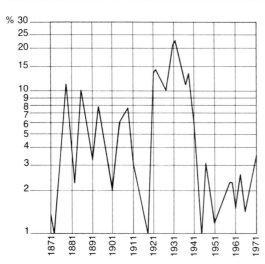

A Graph showing unemployment levels in the UK between 1871 and 1971.

B Cartoon from 'Punch', 5 October 1921.

WORK FOR ALL.

Prime Minister. "COME ON, EVERYBODY, AND LEND A HAND. THIS ISN'T A ONE-MAN JOB!"

C Extract from 'The Road to Wigan Pier' by George Orwell, 1937.

"The total population of Wigan is a little under 87,000 . . . more than one person in three . . . is either drawing or living on the dole . . . And Wigan is not especially badly off as industrial towns go. Even in Sheffield which has been doing well for the last year or so because of wars and rumours of war, the proportion of unemployment is about the same. . . . To study unemployment and its effects you have . . . to go to the industrial areas. In the South unemployment . . . is scattered and queerly unobtrusive [not obvious]. There are plenty of rural districts where a man out of work is almost unheard of. . . ."

D Cartoon from the 'Daily Express', 1936.

Questions

1 *Look at Source* [A] .
  a What does the graph show?
  b What happened to unemployment during the period of: (i) the First World War (1914–18); (ii) the Second World War (1939–45) (iii) between the two World Wars?

2 *Look at Source* [B] .
  a Who or what is the Prime Minister (Lloyd George) trying to save?
  b Can the Government carry out the rescue without help? Explain your answer.
  c Which of the three named onlookers appears most willing and which least willing to help?
  d Do you think the cartoon shows bias in any way? Give reasons for your answer.
  e Explain the connection between the attempt to rescue trade and the title of the cartoon?

3 *Read Source* [C] .
  a In what ways does George Orwell show that he is sympathetic to the plight of the unemployed?
  b What comparisons does Orwell make between the industrial towns and cities in the north of England and the rural districts in the south of England?
  c Sheffield is a steel town. Why had 'wars and rumours of war' affected unemployment there?
  d Would it be useful for an historian to rely on the figures given by George Orwell in Source [C] ? Give reasons for your answer.

4 *Look at Source* [D] .
  a What is the man in the *distressed areas* (areas of high unemployment) looking at?
  b Describe in your own words what is appearing on the horizon. Why is it labelled 'WORK'?
  c Why did rearmament (the manufacture of weapons) offer hope to the unemployed workers in distressed areas?
  d What does the cartoon tell us about the attitude of some people towards rearmament? Why did other people, living at the same time, have a different attitude towards rearmament?
  e Can you tell from the cartoon the social class of the man standing in the distressed areas? Why might this information be important to a social historian?

Linking evidence

5 Source [B] shows efforts to rescue trade and prevent unemployment. From the evidence in Sources [A] and [C] , were the efforts successful in preventing unemployment in the inter-war years?

6 Source [D] offers the unemployed hope for the future. When it was published in 1936 it was described as 'a note of good cheer'. From the evidence in Source [A] , what happened to the level of unemployment in the years after 1936?

7 Which of the Sources is least biased? Give reasons for your choice.

35 The Jarrow Crusade

A **Extract from 'British Economic and Social History, 1700–1982' by C. P. Hill, published in 1985 (Fifth edition).**

". . . The [British] shipbuilding industry . . . from 1930 onwards carried out 'rationalisation' schemes ['rationalizing' an industry means re-organizing it to make it more efficient and cost-effective] . . . to buy up and scrap redundant shipyards. This policy reduced competition and raised prices and so was of little advantage in the overseas market. Its human consequences could be appalling, as was shown by the effects of the closing down of Palmer's Shipyard at Jarrow; in 1935 72 per cent of the workers of the town were unemployed."

B **Extract from 'English Journey' by J. B. Priestley, published in 1934.**

"There is no escape anywhere in Jarrow from its prevailing misery for it is entirely a working class town. One out of every two shops appeared to be permanently closed. Wherever we went there were men hanging about . . . hundreds and thousands of them.

Why had nothing been done about these decaying towns and their workless people?

I know that doles had been given out, Means Tests [a check on a family's sources of income, with a view to setting a level of state benefit payable] applied, training places opened, socks and shirts distributed, but I was not thinking of feeble gestures of that kind."

D **Extract from a letter to the 'Yorkshire Evening Post', 1986.**

"I was listening recently to a radio broadcast about the Jarrow marches . . . surviving men . . . spoke about the kindness shown to them in every town and city they came to . . . one man said that the best reception they got was in Leeds. . . .

The directors of Burton's invited them to their canteen where they were given a good meal of hot soup, meat and potatoes and other vegetables.

Some said they had not tasted meat for weeks because they could not afford it, each marcher was given a complete outfit of clothes . . . suit, boots, underwear. . . .

They were also given a parcel of food and the workers in the canteen made a collection. . . ."

C **Cartoon from the 'Daily Express', 4 November 1936.**

Questions

1 *Read Source* A .
  a Is Source A a primary or a secondary source?
  b What was the effect of the policy of 'rationalization' in British shipbuilding? Did it increase Britain's competitiveness within overseas markets?
  c What were the 'human' consequences of rationalization schemes?

2 *Read Source* B .
  a What was the cause of the misery in Jarrow? Why were men 'hanging about'?
  b Was Priestley sympathetic to the plight of the people of Jarrow or not?
  c Do you feel sympathy for the people living in Jarrow in the 1930s or not? Explain why.

3 *Look at Source* C .
  a The cartoon was entitled 'They travel the road'. From which town had the travellers come?
  b In Europe in 1936 there was a Civil War in Spain; Germany was building up her armed forces; and Italy had alarmed European statesmen by the invasion of Abyssinia in North Africa. How are these problems in Europe shown in the cartoon?
  c The figures in black represent the British politicians and statesmen. In which direction are they looking and why? Do they appear to have noticed the Jarrow Crusade?
  d A crusade can be described as an 'enthusiastic campaign for a cause'. What was the cause of the Jarrow marchers, and why was it described as a crusade?
  e Can you see any evidence in the cartoon to indicate that the 'crusaders' tried to keep up their spirits on the march?

4 *Read Source* D .
  a The men on the 1936 Crusade marched from Jarrow to London with a petition for the politicians in Parliament. How were the men treated in the towns and cities through which they passed on their route?
  b Do you think the directors and the workers at Burton's sympathized with the marchers on the Jarrow Crusade or not? What evidence in Source D supports your answer?
  c How useful do you think this Source would be for an historian?
  d What problems might the evidence pose for an historian?
  e If you had been living at the time, how would you have received the Jarrow marchers? Write a letter to a newspaper describing your feelings and your memories of the day when the marchers arrived in your town.

Linking evidence

5 Jarrow became known as the 'town that was murdered'. Can you suggest why?

6 Using Sources C and D compare the way in which the cartoonist (Source C) has shown the reaction of the politicians to the Jarrow Crusade, with the way in which ordinary people reacted to the marchers (Source D).

7 What information or attitudes is the cartoonist (Source C) able to include which a photograph could not?

36.1 The cotton industry in the twentieth century

A Weaving in Rochdale, Lancashire, around 1910.

B Weaving in the 1930s.

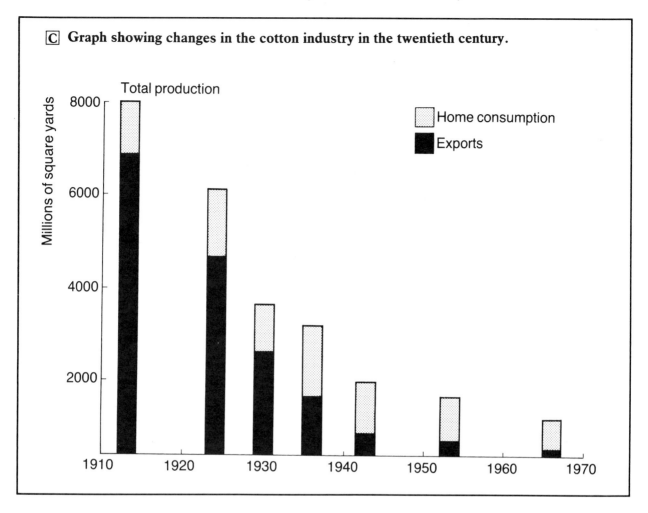

C Graph showing changes in the cotton industry in the twentieth century.

Questions

1 *Look at Sources* A *and* B .
  a What type of sources are Sources A and B , and what do they show?
  b What do you notice about the workers in both illustrations?
  c How do you think the younger weavers were taught to operate the looms?
  d What period of time (approximate number of years) separates the two illustrations?
  e Make a list of all the similarities and differences between the two scenes. In what ways do they provide evidence of continuity? In what ways do they provide evidence of change?
  f How do Sources A and B provide evidence of the lack of progress of the cotton inudstry?
  g How might the two illustrations assist an historian in trying to find out what happened to the cotton industry in the early decades of the twentieth century?
  h What problems does the evidence pose for an historian?

2 *Look at Source* C .
  a In which year did the United Kingdom manufacture and export most cotton cloth?
  b What happened to Britain's exports of cotton cloth during and after the Second World War (1939–45)?
  c What happened to the total production of cotton cloth between 1938 and 1940?
  d The figures show an increase in the amount of cotton cloth used in the UK in the late 1930s and early 1940s (though the total produced fell). Can you suggest why this might be?

36.2 The cotton industry in the twentieth century

D **Opinion of the owner of a spinning firm in the 1920s.**
"We were struggling desperately, financially and commercially, from an appalling depression . . . the mill masters conceived that there wasn't the sort of money around, to indulge in massive capital expenditure."

E **Opinion of a Lancashire cotton mill manager in the 1940s, quoted in 'All Our Working Lives' by P. Pagnamenta and R. Overy, published in 1984.**
". . . As for thoughts of re-equipping, with all that disturbance, and disruption of production, you just don't want to know about it."

F **Extract from the 'Report of the Cotton Textile Mission to the United States', published by the Ministry of Production in 1944.**
"The United States industry is very far ahead of Lancashire in production per man-hour. . . . The machinery employed throughout is more modern, and methods about which our industry is in doubt have become general practice."

G **Recollections of a resident in a Lancashire mill town, quoted in 'All Our Working Lives' by P. Pagnamenta and R. Overy, published in 1984.**
"I remember my wife coming home one day with a jersey, not cotton, that she'd bought for the lad. And I looked at it, and it said 'Made in Hong Kong'. So I threw it in the coal fire. . . . She said: 'Well I couldn't afford a British one'. I said: 'Well, he'll do without'."

H **The reaction of a skilled spinner to the situation after the Cotton Industry Act of 1959 which empowered the Government to close down old works and** offer generous grants to owners who decided to modernize, quoted in 'All Our Working Lives' by P. Pagnamenta and R. Overy, published in 1984.
"They broke them all up, scrapped 'em and sold them for scrap that's all they did, just broke them up with a sledge hammer. We were the last three mules [type of spinning machine], to be running. The others were hit with a big hammer, and it's heartbreaking to see it being done because you looked after them mules like they were your own child really."

I **Opinion of Robert Porter, manager of a spinning firm.**
"I believe that the main reason was the conservative attitude of the men in charge, the employers in general who did not face the issue of re-equipment when all the signs were there that they should have done . . . they should have installed more modern machinery in the thirties, forties and fifties. . . ."

J **Viewpoint of some Lancashire managers.**
"There was a great deal that could have been done by a more vigorous attack by the government of the day on the problems with the import situation."

K **An opinion from Lancashire expressed shortly after the company Courtaulds closed their factory at Skelmerdale and describing the situation in the 1960s and 1970s, quoted in 'All Our Working Lives' by P. Pagnamenta and R. Overy, published in 1984.**
". . . no matter how efficient, how productive, how up to date the machinery is, our wage structure in this country is so much higher than the cheap low-cost countries abroad that we still couldn't see it being successful."

3 *Read Sources* [D] , [E] , [F] , [G] , [H] *and* [I] .

   a Why do you think the author of Source [G] objected to his son wearing a garment made in Hong Kong?

   b According to Source [I] when should modern machinery have been installed in the cotton mills? According to Sources [D] and [E] , why wasn't it?

   c Since the Second World War, Japan and a number of other Far Eastern countries had been modernizing their methods of production. Which other country also used more modern machinery than Britain?

   d What happened to much of the outdated machinery after the Cotton Industry Act of 1959?

4 Sources [D] – [K] provide evidence of some of the reasons for the decline of the cotton industry in the twentieth century. Which Sources provide evidence that the decline was due to:

   (i) failure to modernize machinery;

   (ii) competition from abroad;

   (iii) availability of 'non cotton fibres';

   (iv) high wages in the industry;

   (v) failure of the Government to control imports?

5 Using Sources [D] – [K] which trace the decline of the cotton industry:

   (i) Who do the employers blame?

   (ii) Who do the Government blame?

   (iii) Who might the workers blame?

   (iv) Who do you blame?

Linking evidence

6 In 1939 a Lancashire cotton manufacturer recorded that 'When I came into the industry in 1939 we had still got the machinery that my grandfather purchased in 1906'. Which of the Sources [A] – [K] indicate that there had been few major changes in cotton textile machinery in the early twentieth century?

7 Which of the Sources ([A] – [K]) comes closest to *proving* that the cotton industry had declined by the 1930s?

8 Rayon, Nylon and Terylene are examples of synthetic or man-made fibres. How would the growth of these industries in Britain and abroad affect the United Kingdom cotton industry?

9 It was often stated that the Lancashire weaving looms were so strongly built that they would last sixty years. What were the main advantages and disadvantages of such lasting equipment?

10 Using Sources [A] – [K] write an account of how the changing fortunes of the cotton industry affected a weaver between 1913 (when she was 14 years old) and 1959 (when she finally retired). Use the following pairs of words: 'I thought'; 'I believed'; 'I feared'; 'I hoped'.

37 Evacuation

A Poster issued by the British Government in 1939.

B Poster issued by the Ministry of Health.

C Extract from the reminiscences of a headteacher, taken from 'Brodsworth Centenary 1871–1971'.

"*Evacuation to Brodsworth*

1939 Evacuation of children . . . Highfields school . . . used as Reception Centre . . . commenced the billeting of these children [arranging for each child to have a home to go to] from Leeds Quarry Hill Flats. . . .

The next day, it was the turn of the Mothers and babies. The main question asked was 'Where is the fish & chips shop and the Pub'. They were not pleased to be denied these facilities, I'm afraid by the end of a fortnight of country life they preferred to go back to Leeds and risk the German bombs. . . . Eventually town and country children settled down and became friends and school work proceeded . . . 1940 . . . Air-raid sirens occasionally sounded in school hours, we had only . . . a stirrup pump and two buckets of water for dealing with incendiary bombs [bombs which start fires]. . . ."

D An evacuee remembers in 'One Child's War' by Victoria Massey, published in 1978.

"It turned out that we were to be evacuated . . . to Wales. . . . A trail of mothers and children with bags and gas masks slung over shoulders, and with packages under arms, labels flapping in buttonholes, made their way along the dock road towards the village school. . . We were bustled . . . into the coach, and told to hold on to our luggage, and gazed down from our seats to our mothers below. My own mother . . . smiled up at us but with a desperate look as though she was within two minds . . . not let us go at all. . . .

My mother mouthed some words but I could see she dared not shout for fear of weeping. . . ."

Questions

1 *Look at Sources* A *and* B .
  a What type of source are Sources A and B ? When were they published and by whom?
  b Sources A and B have a common theme. Is it: (i) orphans; (ii) evacuation; (iii) boarding schools; or (iv) homelessness?
  c Does the advice in Source B support or contradict the advice in Source A ?
  d What does Source A advise London mothers to do with their children?
  e The children shown in Source B have been evacuated to the country. (i) What is the mother tempted to do? (ii) What is she advised to do by the Ministry of Health?

2 *Read Source* C .
  a What evidence in Source C indicates the reason for the evacuation?
  b Was evacuation to the country a guarantee of total safety from air-raids and bombing?
  c In what ways would Source C be useful to an historian?
  d In what ways might this evidence pose problems for an historian?
  e Why did some people return to their homes?

3 *Read Source* D .
  a Would you describe the extract as a primary or a secondary source? Explain your answer.
  b Which three of the following words do you consider would best describe the behaviour and actions of the mothers and children in Source D : brave, uncaring, sad, happy, selfish, sensible, thoughtless, cheerful, responsible?

Linking evidence

4 Is there any evidence in Sources C and D to show that some mothers followed the advice given in Source A ?

5 Is there any evidence in Source C to indicate that some mothers did not follow the advice given in Source B ?

6 Why might the situation as described in Sources C and D create the need for a poster such as Source B ?

38 Colonial and New Commonwealth immigration

A **Extract from an article in 'The Times', 13 November 1941, quoting the Secretary of State for the Colonies.**
"A great expansion had taken place in our African troops, and tens of thousands of men of the African races now supplied man-power . . . each week we welcomed . . . parties of volunteers . . . to join the R.A.F. and other fighting units. We had also been reinforced by hundreds of technicians, timber workers and skilled personnel.

The great resources of man-power available in the Colonial Empire must be used not only for the war effort but in the constructive work of peace-time development."

B **Extract from an article in 'The Times', 2 December 1941.**
"A luncheon at the West Indian Club . . . was made the occasion of warm tributes to the many men and women of our African and West Indian Dependencies who are giving generous and spontaneous service in the Empire's war effort. . . . We had had hundreds of highly skilled technicians from the West Indies and Africa, thousands of seamen who were continually facing the terrible dangers of submarines, hundreds from the West Indies who had come over to join the Royal Air Force."

C **Oral evidence of Linette Simms, who became a school bus driver in England.**
". . . Work was very hard to find in Jamaica. So the only way I could think out was to leave my country and travel out.

I came here because I thought it would be better than my homeland. If things were good there I wouldn't have come here in the first place. I came here in 1953 on my own. . . ."

D **Extract from an article in 'The Times', 4 August 1965.**
"The Midlands is more dependent on immigrant labour than anywhere else in Britain. In the hot and heavy industries such as foundries – never popular in times of full employment with the home labour force – they frequently constitute the only available pool of labour. So well have they adapted themselves to the work . . . that some firms express a preference for immigrants . . . the largest immigrant community in the north is centred on Bradford and the wool-textile industry. Large numbers of them man nightshifts – it has been claimed that nightshifts would be forced to close down entirely without them. . . ."

E **Extract from 'My Life' by Sir Oswald Mosley, published in 1968. (Oswald Mosley founded the British Union of Fascists in October 1932).**
". . . Jamaican immigrants . . . were driven to Britain by the lash of starvation, and their arrival created inevitably a still more acute housing shortage, coupled with the threat of unemployment to British people if the competition for jobs became more acute in industrial crisis.

My proposal was simply to repatriate immigrants to their homeland with fares paid and to fulfil the Government's pledge to buy sugar from Jamaica . . . which would have restored that island to prosperity. . . ."

F **Extract from a speech by Enoch Powell, MP, at Birmingham 1968.**
"In fifteen or twenty years, on present trends, there will be in this country 3½ million Commonwealth immigrants and their descendants. . . . Whole areas . . . will be occupied by immigrant and immigrant-descended population. . . . The first question for a nation . . . is to ask: How can its dimensions be reduced?. . . . The answers . . . are by stopping, or virtually stopping, further inflow, and by promoting the maximum outflow."

Questions

1 *Read Sources* A *and* B .

a Why had large numbers of colonial immigrants come to Britain during the early 1940s?

b Give two examples of colonies from which they came.

c In what ways did the colonial immigrants contribute to the war effort?

d Do you agree that the contribution of colonial immigrants to the war effort was generous? Did the colonials *have* to fight for Britain during the war? What word in Source A might be used in an answer to both these questions?

2 *Study Sources* C *and* D .

a Why did many people leave Jamaica (in the West Indies) and come to Britain in the 1950s?

b What kinds of work was undertaken by immigrants who came to Britain in the 1950s and 1960s? Give more than one example.

c Why did some British firms express a preference for immigrant labour?

d It has been said that without the contribution of immigrant doctors and nurses in the 1960s the National Health Service could not have kept going. What evidence in Sources C and D suggests that immigrant labour was also essential to British transport and industry?

3 *Read Sources* E *and* F .

a What fears are expressed in Sources E and F about immigration?

b What did the authors of Sources E and F propose?

c What do Sources E and F tell you about the attitude of some people towards immigration?

d In what ways might the evidence in Sources E and F be useful to an historian trying to find out about immigration?

e Is Source F concerned with the *short-term* or the *long-term* effects of immigration? What evidence supports your answer?

Linking evidence

4 Would you say that the evidence (Sources A – F) selected for this section: (i) was *biased* in favour of immigration; (ii) gave a *balanced* view of immigration; (iii) presented a *positive* view of immigration; or (iv) gave a *negative* view of immigration? Explain your answer, quoting from the Sources to support your view.

5 Does Source E agree in *any way* with the evidence in Sources C and D ?

6 In what ways do the Sources provide evidence to suggest that immigrants were:

(i) welcomed into Britain when their services and skills were needed;

(ii) made less welcome when their skills and services were not in great demand?

7 Why might the evidence selected in this section (A –F) present problems for an historian?

8 Which of the Sources A – F seems to be the least biased? Explain your answer.

9 Give an example of *opinion* from each of *three* of the Sources.

39 Post-war housing

A **Extract from 'Changing Horizons: Britain 1914–80' by W. O. Simpson, published in 1986.**

"Bombing had destroyed or damaged thousands of dwellings and there were still large areas in the England of the first industrial revolution where slums needed to be cleared. Skilled manpower and building materials were in short supply so that house-building inevitably got away to a slow start. Bevan [Minister of Housing, 1945–51] concentrated his efforts on encouraging local authorities to add to their stocks of council housing. . . . A Housing Production Executive was also set up in April 1946. The pace of construction increased from 139000 houses completed in 1947 to 227000 in 1948. The total number of houses built between August 1945 and December 1951 reached 1016349. The annual average figure was well below the target of 300000 houses a year which Churchill set for Macmillan in 1951, but it was still no mean achievement. . . ."

PREVENTION IS BETTER . . .

(Estimated additional expenditure on National Health Services for 1950—£129 millions Proposed reduction in expenditure on Housing for 1950—£24 millions)

B **Cartoon from 'Punch', 5 April 1950.**

D **Extract from an article in 'The Times', October 1969.**

"Out of a total stock of 17,300,000 houses in England, Wales and Scotland, less than ten million according to government standards have basic sanitary amenities [facilities]. Of the remainder over two million are 'unfit' and must be demolished, 2,500,000 are sub-standard and not worth improving and, according to the Ministry of Housing, will also have to be demolished, and a further 2,500,000 are sub-standard and require improvements and repairs."

C **Varieties of post-war housing.**

Questions

1 *Read Source* A .
   a Source A includes both *short-term* and *long-term* reasons for the serious housing problem in Britain since the 1940s. Give one example of each.
   b The Second World War ended in 1945. Can you suggest why there was a shortage of skilled manpower and building materials at that time?
   c What were the effects of these shortages on the house-building programme?
   d Which category of housing, council or private, was mainly encouraged after 1945?
   e From the evidence in Source A , give one *fact* and one *opinion* implied by the author.

2 *Look at Source* B .
   a How does the cartoonist show that the area was run down and decaying?
   b A long queue has formed. Where have the people in the queue come from?
   c Which building are they waiting to enter? How does it contrast with the other buildings?
   d The caption to the cartoon is incomplete. The missing words are 'than cure'. Why is this a suitable caption for this cartoon?
   e What connection is the cartoonist trying to make between housing conditions and health?
   f In 1950 it was proposed to reduce the amount of money spent on housing by £24 million and to increase the amount spent on the National Health Service by £129 million. Can you explain the connection between this information and the attitude of the cartoonist?

3 *Look at Source* C .
   a Source C shows two methods of providing dwellings in the years after the Second World War. Identify and describe: (i) the prefabricated ('prefab') dwellings (c. 1945); (ii) the high-rise flats (c. 1959). Can you explain why the prefabs were erected *before* the flats?
   b Can you suggest:
      (i) some of the advantages of *building* these types of dwellings; (ii) some of the disadvantages of *living* in these types of dwellings?

4 *Read Source* D .
   a Are the following *true* or *false*?
      (i) In 1969 ten million houses in England, Wales and Scotland lacked basic sanitary facilities.
      (ii) In 1969 four and a half million houses needed to be demolished.
      (iii) In 1969 five million houses were sub-standard.
      (iv) In 1969 two million houses were 'unfit' for human habitation and required improvements and repairs.

Linking evidence

5 In October 1986, the Prince of Wales said he believed that 'leaving the inner cities to fester results in an ever-increasing spiral of decay, of poor physical and mental health and general low morale. . . .' (*The Observer*, 2 November 1986). How might this statement be used to support the argument that the attitude of the cartoonist in *Punch* in 1950 (Source B) is still relevant today?

6 In January 1987 Lord Scarman said he believed that 'Tomorrow our own children and grandchildren will find themselves condemned to live in slums unless something is done now' (*The Observer*). How might this statement (and the information in Source D) be used to support the argument that slum clearance has been and remains a long-term problem?

7 Which of the Sources A – D might be used to argue the case *for* the need for slum clearance? Give *two* examples.

40 The National Health Service

A Extract from Clause 1 of the National Health Service Act, 1946.

"It shall be the duty of the Minister of Health to promote the establishment . . . of a comprehensive health service designed to secure improvement in the physical and mental health of the people. . . ."

B Extract from 'British Economic and Social History 1700–1982' by C. P. Hill, published in 1985 (Fifth edition).

". . . the establishment of the National Health Service . . . aroused . . . controversy; partly because the doctors disliked the idea that they should become in some degree servants of the state. . . . The scheme provided that every kind of medical, optical and dental treatment should be available without charge to every member of the community. Costs were to be met out of taxation. Those who wished could pay for private doctors and private treatment. Within twelve months 95 per cent of the population had joined the scheme. Another important element was the reorganisation of hospitals under regional boards. . . . Millions obtained attention and treatment – spectacles, dental services, drugs, minor operations – which they had needed but not been able to afford. . . . It cost far more than had been anticipated, largely because of the backlog of hidden demand."

NO, NO, NO! WRONG ADDRESS, I TELL YOU!

D Cartoon by David Low, 1948.

E Extract from the 'Daily Mail', 5 July 1948.

"On Monday morning you will wake in a new Britain, in a state which takes over its citizens six months before they are born, providing free care and services for their early years, their schooling, sickness, workless days, widowhood and retirement. Finally, it helps defray [off-set] the cost of their departures. All this with free doctoring, dentistry and medicine – free bath chairs [large, wheeled chairs for invalids], too, if needed – for four and eleven pence [25p] of your weekly pay packet."

HERE HE COMES, BOYS!

C Cartoon from 'News Chronicle', 7 August 1945.

Questions

1 *Read Source* A .
a Aneurin Bevan (Minister of Health and Housing, 1945–51) believed that 'Society becomes more wholesome . . . if . . . its citizens have . . . the knowledge that not only themselves but all their fellows have access when ill to the best that medical science can provide. . .'. **How did the National Health Service Act of 1946 help to put such beliefs into practice?**
b What was the main purpose of the Health Service?

2 *Read Source* B .
a How can you tell this is a secondary source?
b Which group of people opposed the establishment of the National Health Service, and why?
c Did the establishment of the National Health Service mean the end of private medicine?
d Why might the medical profession want private medicine to continue?
e In 1948, one general practitioner (doctor) commented 'One would think the people saved up their illnesses for the first free day'. According to Source B : (i) Why had so many people not sought treatment before the National Health Service came into effect? (ii) How did this rush for treatment effect the cost of the new Health Service?

3 *Look at Sources* C *and* D .
a What type of sources are Sources C and D ?
b In both Sources what is Aneurin Bevan, the Minister for Health, carrying in his hand?
c Harley Street in London (Source C) is famous for private medicine. What was the attitude of these doctors to the new Minister of Health and what were they planning to do to his 'health for all scheme'?
d In Source D what were 'Dr Bevan' and the 'midwife' trying to deliver to the BMA (British Medical Association)?
e In Source D what is the attitude of the BMA to the National Health Service Act? Would you describe it as welcoming or hostile? Explain your answer.
f What do the dates of Sources C and D tell you about the period over which some doctors opposed the new Health Service proposals?

4 *Read Source* E .
a Which Act came into effect on Monday 5 July 1948?
b The Welfare State is sometimes described as providing support from 'the cradle to the grave'. What evidence in Source E supports that description?

Linking evidence

5 From the evidence in Sources A – E can you suggest which people were likely to benefit most from the new National Health Service, and why?

6 Aneurin Bevan wrote a book called *In Place of Fear*. How might the National Health Service remove some of the fears of British men and women?

7 Why did some doctors dislike the policies of Aneurin Bevan, the Minister of Health?

8 On 5 July 1948 *The Times* wrote of the new Welfare State: 'Can the next generation reap the benefits of a social service State while avoiding the perils of a Santa Claus State?'. Can you list the main advantages and disadvantages of the Welfare State?

9 Why do you think some people argue that today the Welfare State means that as a nation 'we have it too easy'?

41 Modern motorways

A **Extract from 'Post-War Planning and Reconstruction' by the Institution of Municipal and County Engineers, published in 1942.**

"Motorways are the best means of providing rapid and safe road transport. Their construction would in many cases cost less, and require less land, and interfere less with amenities [facilities], than the adaptation of existing routes to the dual-carriageway system. . . . During their construction there would be little interference with traffic, and they would provide additional road space. . . .

Only the most important roads would be linked up with a motorway, by suitably designed junctions . . . all minor roads being carried under or over the motorway by bridges. The motorways would by-pass the large towns, to which access would be provided by junctions. . . .

Mechanical plant [machinery] suitable for road making, of which there has been a large increase in connection with aerodrome construction, would enable the work to be carried out quickly and with economy."

C **Extract from 'New Society', 31 October 1986.**

"DID WE REALLY NEED THE M25?

The final section of the M25, London's 117 mile [188 km] orbital motorway, was opened by the prime minister on Wednesday. It has taken 13 years to build, and the best part of this century to plan; the idea of a ringway round London first emerged as long ago as 1905.

The motorway has been expensive – not merely because of the estimated £1,000 million it cost to build, but also in terms of its effect on the environment . . . 221 of the 228 acres required for the road were green belt. . . .

That the motorway would have its costs has never been denied. But its supporters maintain that these are outweighed by the benefits . . . quicker journey times for users and greatly relieved congestion on neighbouring roads.

Many . . . groups, however, argue that the M25 . . . in generating a greatly increased volume of traffic . . . has created new congestion and other difficulties. . . ."

B Photograph showing the viaduct which carries the South Wales motorway into London.

Questions

1 *Read Source* A .

  a What is Source A and when was it written?

  b Would you describe Source A as: (i) biased in favour of motorways; (ii) biased against motorways; or (iii) a fair and unbiased assessment? Quote from the Source to support your answer.

  c What arguments are put forward to support the case for the development of motorways?

  d Does Source A give the impression that in 1942: (i) some motorways were already in existence; or (ii) motorways were a new idea?

  e Source A suggests that motorways would by-pass the large towns. What advantages and disadvantages would this bring to the by-passed towns?

  f Why had there been a large increase in the sort of mechanical equipment which would be suitable for building roads?

2 *Look at Source* B .

  a Photographs can only show one particular place at one moment in time. Motorways have existed in Britain for thirty years and there are now more than 3000 kilometres of motorway. What is the value of a photograph as historical evidence?

  b Describe briefly how: (i) vehicles join the motorway; (ii) vehicles leave the motorway.

  c What feature, shown in the photograph, assists the motorist to find his or her direction?

3 *Read Source* C .

  a Is Source C a primary or a secondary source? Explain your answer. Does this mean that an historian would find it less useful than Source A ?

  b What did those who *supported* the building of the orbital motorway around London believe would be the *benefit* of the M25?

  c What did those who *opposed* its construction believe would be the *effects* of the M25?

Linking evidence

4 Source C is entitled 'Did We Really Need the M25?' What is your opinion?

5 Source A forecast that the cost of constructing motorways would be less than that required for improving existing roads. Does the evidence in Source C support or contradict this view?

6 Source A was written in 1942. The motorway shown in Source B was constructed thirty years later. What features of motorways forecast in Source A can you identify in Source B ?

7 Consider all the arguments in Sources A – C *for* and *against* motorways. In your opinion which case is most convincing?

8 In what ways does Source C show a different attitude to that expressed in Source A ?

42 New technology

B Extract from an article, 'Economic progress in Britain in the 1920s', by D. H. Aldcroft and published in 1966 in 'Scottish Journal of Political Economy'.
". . . perhaps for the first time businessmen were brought face to face with the grim reality that they had to adopt more scientific methods of production and reorganise their plant and equipment on more efficient lines. . . ."

THE SAVING OF LABOUR.

THE ROBOT. "MASTER, I CAN DO THE WORK OF FIFTY MEN."
EMPLOYER. "YES. I KNOW THAT. BUT *WHO IS TO SUPPORT THE FIFTY MEN?*"

A Cartoon from 'Punch', January 1933.

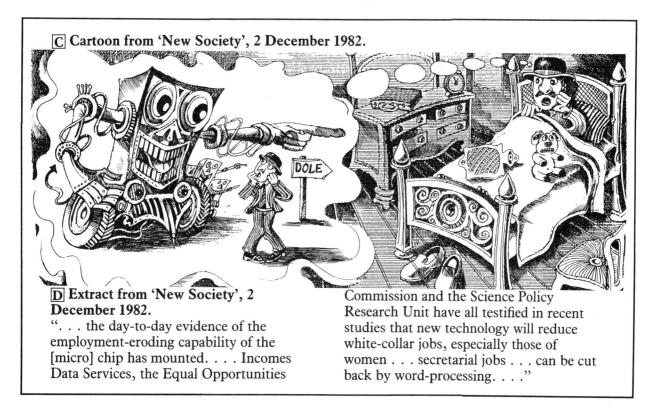

C Cartoon from 'New Society', 2 December 1982.

D Extract from 'New Society', 2 December 1982.
". . . the day-to-day evidence of the employment-eroding capability of the [micro] chip has mounted. . . . Incomes Data Services, the Equal Opportunities Commission and the Science Policy Research Unit have all testified in recent studies that new technology will reduce white-collar jobs, especially those of women . . . secretarial jobs . . . can be cut back by word-processing. . . ."

Questions

1 *Look at Sources* A *and* B.
   a To which period in history do both Sources relate: (i) before the First World War; (ii) after the Second World War; or (iii) the inter-war years?
   b What two characters are shown in Source A, and what are they 'talking' about?
   c Explain the connection (Source A) between: (i) the papers labelled Labour Costs, Wages, Output on the desk; and (ii) the offer made by the robot.
   d Why might the employer be tempted to accept the robot's offer? Why might the employer decide to refuse the offer?
   e What evidence in Source B indicates that other employers and businessmen faced similar problems to those shown in the cartoon (Source A)?

2 *Look at Sources* C *and* D.
   a According to Sources C and D which type of employment is threatened by the development of new technology?
   b Why has the man in Source C woken up?
   c Does the robot represent (i) new technology; (ii) the Government; (iii) the employer?

Linking evidence

3 Sources A and C have a common theme. What is it?

4 The cartoons A and C indicate the possible threat to employment by new manufacturing methods and new technology. Which Source, in your opinion, makes this point most strongly?

5 Why should an historian look at other evidence besides the cartoons A and C before forming an opinion on the effects of the new technology?

43 Science and society

A **Extract from the Norman Lockyer Lecture given by the scientist Ernest Rutherford in 1936.**

"During the last few years, there has been much loose and uninformed talk of the possible dangers to the community of the unrestricted development of science and scientific invention. Taking a broad view, I think that it cannot be denied that the progress of scientific knowledge has so far been overwhelmingly beneficial to the welfare of mankind. . . . It is, of course, true that some of the advances of Science may occasionally be used for ignoble ends, but this is not the fault of the scientific man but rather of the community which fails to control this prostitution of Science. . . . It is sometimes suggested that scientific men should be more active in controlling the wrong use of their discoveries. I am doubtful, however, whether even the most imaginative scientific man except in rare cases is able to foresee the ultimate effect of any discovery. . . ."

B **Cartoon from the 'Evening Standard', 4 June 1946.**

"BABY PLAY WITH NICE BALL?"

C **Cartoon by Sir David Low.**

D **Cartoon by Vicky, 1954.**

HARNESSING THE ATOM

"Of course I know what I'm doing . . ."

Questions

1 *Read Source* A.

   a Rutherford was the first person to split the atom. Did he believe that scientists should be responsible for the use made of their discoveries?

   b Why did he think it would be difficult for scientists to control the use of their discoveries?

   c Would you describe the evidence in Source A as *fact* or *opinion*? Explain why.

   d Do you agree or disagree with the view expressed? Give reasons for your answer.

2 *Look at Source* B.

   a What is the form of energy shown in Source B?

   b How has the cartoonist indicated that it is a powerful form of energy?

   c What do the two men represent?

   d Explain the connection between the title of the cartoon and the objects the men are holding.

3 *Look at Source* C.

   a Is the adult figure drawn to represent a scientist or a politician?

   b What does he have in his pocket?

   c What is the 'baby' meant to represent?

   d What is the 'nice ball' the baby is being given to play with?

   e Can you explain why the 'ball' is labelled 'Life or Death'?

   f In your own words explain the message that the cartoonist is trying to get across. (Note: Three days before the cartoon appeared, the first atomic bomb had been exploded on the Japanese city of Hiroshima.)

4 *Look at Sources* C *and* D.

   a What has the 'ball' the baby was offered in Source C become in Source D?

   b What do the cartoonists of Sources C and D suggest about the mental age of humanity?

   c What might happen if the baby shown in Source D dropped the 'ball'?

   d Explain how the cartoonist's view of the mental age of humanity might contradict the caption of the cartoon (Source D).

Linking evidence

5 Sources A – D have a common theme. What is it?

6 In what ways do the Sources provide evidence to suggest that: (i) some scientific development may be difficult to control; (ii) some scientific developments are too dangerous to be placed in the hands of mankind; (iii) mankind has a responsible attitude for the use of any and every scientific discovery?

7 Do you consider any of the evidence in Sources A – D to be biased? Explain your answer.

8 Do you think the cartoonists of Sources C and D approved of the 'scientist' giving his 'discovery' to 'mankind'? Explain your answer.

9 Do you think there is sufficient information in Sources A – D for *you* to make a judgement on what is the *right* or *wrong* use of atomic energy? Give reasons to support your answer.

44.1 Changing forms of energy

A Cartoon in 'Punch', 25 January 1881.

B Cartoon in 'Punch', December 1935.

" WHAT WILL HE GROW TO?"

WANTED—A FAIRY GODMOTHER.

CINDERELLA (*sadly*). "AFTER ALL, I DO THE ROUGH WORK FOR BOTH OF THEM."

C **Sir Alan Cottrell FRS, a member of the UK Atomic Energy Authority, writing in 'The Observer' in 1986.**

"The Case for Nuclear Power in Britain
. . . because oil and gas are plentiful today, they will [*not*] always . . . be readily available . . . North Sea production . . . will be well down at the end of the century and Britain will be forced to import energy . . . from World markets in which oil, gas and coal prices will be shooting up rapidly. . . .

. . . even if Britain aims at only a modest rate of economic growth . . . then by the year 2020 . . . our energy consumption will have practically to double. . . .

. . . some decades are needed to build a great new energy industry of a size to match our future needs. . . . There is no practical possibility of output from our coal, hydro-electric and renewable energy resources being able to expand to anything like the level necessary. . . .

The only way, then . . . will be to meet most of the short-fall with nuclear power . . . there is another reason why Britain should develop more nuclear power. . . . It will surely be right for advanced industrial countries, such as Britain, to limit their demands for the world's remaining fossil fuel resources [oil, gas, coal] in order to leave as much as possible for the third world. . . ."

Questions

1 *Look at Source* [A] .
  a What is the subject of the cartoon?
  b Three forms of energy are shown. What are they?
  c Which two forms of energy has the cartoonist shown as 'Kings'? Why?
  d Which form of energy is shown as the 'baby'? Can you explain why?
  e The cartoonist suggests that 'Electricity' has an advantage. What is it?
  f What might happen to steam and coal if electricity 'grew'?
  g Write down in your own words what you think is the message of the cartoonist.

2 *Look at Source* [B] .
  a On which fairy story is the cartoon based?
  b Which forms of energy are shown as 'the ugly sisters'?
  c Which form of energy is shown as Cinderella? Can you suggest why?
  d The cartoonist is commenting on the relationship between coal, gas and electricity. Is the cartoonist saying that: (i) gas and electricity are cleaner and better than coal or (ii) coal is used to produce both gas and electricity or (iii) gas and electricity are more expensive forms of energy than coal.

3 *Read Source* [C] .
  a According to the author of Source [C] , why will the fossil fuels (oil, gas, coal) be unable to meet all of Britain's energy needs by the end of the century?
  b Does the author expect Britain's energy consumption to have *increased* or *decreased* by the year 2020?
  c What source of energy does Source [C] suggest as an alternative to the use of fossil fuels?
  d What arguments are put forward to support the case for the development of nuclear energy?
  e Why might the development of nuclear energy in Britain help the Third World?
  f What evidence in Source [C] suggest that long-term planning is necessary to meet future energy needs?

4 *Look at Sources* [A] , [B] *and* [C] .
  a What period of time (how many years) separates each of the Sources [A] , [B] and [C] ?
  b In what ways does the cartoon (Source [B]) add to the information in Source [A] about the changing relationship between coal and electricity?
  c Are Sources [A] and [B] primary or secondary sources?
  d What is the value of such cartoons as historical sources?
  e In Source [B] coal was used to produce gas. How does Source [C] indicate that gas can now be obtained in other ways?
  f Using Sources [A] , [B] , [C] write a brief description of some of the changes which have taken place over the last one hundred years in the forms of energy used and explain how and why these have occurred.
  g From Sources [A] , [B] , [C] can you give one example of a *cause* of change and one example of a *result* of change?

44.2   Changing forms of energy

D **Extract from 'Click', published by British Nuclear Fuels in 1986.**
"Any exposure of employees or the general public to radiation . . . is strictly controlled. . . .

In fact, radioactive materials associated with nuclear electricity generation account for an extremely small proportion of all the radioactivity which is in our environment . . . just over 0.1 per cent. . . .

. . . by the early 1990s emissions of long-lived radiation from Sellafield [nuclear power station in the north-west of England] will be reduced to less than one per cent of peak levels. Extensive monitoring programmes are carried out at each site involving many thousands of samples a year of such things as milk, seafoods, air and water to ensure that radiation doses due to discharges remain a small fraction of recommended limits . . . the nuclear energy industry is one of the safest industries in the world, thanks to the design, construction and operation of plant [factory and/or machinery] with safety in mind. . . ."

E **Extract from 'I love nuclear power (but not in my back yard)' by Rob Edwards, published in the 'New Statesman', 7 March 1986.**
"Sellafield's [nuclear power station in the north-west of England] safety record is undeniably appalling. There have been a total of 270 accidents at the plant since 1950, the most serious in 1957 causing three million gallons of contaminated milk from nearby farms to be poured away. After a series of leaks in the late 1970s, the government's Health and Safety Executive conducted a major safety review which said that the plant's [the factory's] safety standards had 'deteriorated to an unsatisfactory level'. . . .

. . . BNFL (British Nuclear Fuels Limited which now runs Sellafield) were successfully prosecuted by the government for the incidents which led to the contamination of local beaches in 1983 and 1984. In the last two months there have been four significant mishaps at Sellafield. . . ."

F **Extract from 'Burying a Nuclear Waste Policy', the editorial in 'The Independent', 2 May 1987.**
"OF THE MANY contentious activities associated with the development of civil nuclear power, the disposal of radioactive waste is the one where . . . no matter how many times the nuclear industry proclaims the 'basic safety' . . . of its . . . disposal . . . the public . . . refuses to believe it.

. . . public concern cannot be ignored. Electricity cannot be generated at nuclear power plants without the production of significant volumes of long-lasting radioactive waste. Any Government which . . . has committed itself to the expansion of civil nuclear power can only proceed on the basis that it has a publicly acceptable policy for . . . disposing of all such waste.

. . . the Government is running away . . . from the political pitfalls of its nuclear waste policy. . . . In the past two years, it has . . . abandoned plans for burying the waste on an industrial site at Billingham . . . to store intermediate as well as low-level waste in shallow inland burial sites, and . . . chucked over . . . four low-level waste sites as well. . . ."

5 *Read Source* D .
   a Is Source D a primary or a secondary source? Explain your answer.
   b What percentage of the total amount of radiation in the environment is due to the generation of electricity by nuclear power?
   c What efforts are made by British Nuclear Fuels to limit and check the amount of radiation in the environment?

6 *Read Source* E .
   a What type of power is used to generate electricity at Sellafield?
   b Why might Source E make some people fear nuclear power?
   c In what ways had radiation leaked from the nuclear power station at Sellafield?
   d The world's first industrial-scale power station was opened at Calder Hall on the Sellafield site in 1956. Why might this information cast doubt on some of the evidence in Source E ?

7 *Read Source* F .
   a What type of 'waste' is produced at nuclear power stations?
   b Why are people concerned about the disposal of waste from nuclear power stations?
   c Why is it important for the Government to have a policy for the disposal of radioactive waste which is acceptable to the general public?
   d What plans for the disposal of radioactive waste have already been considered and abandoned?

Linking evidence

8 Which of the Sources C – F :
   (i) support the case for the development of nuclear power;
   (ii) oppose the development of nuclear power?

9 From Sources C – F select three arguments *in favour of* nuclear power and three arguments *against* nuclear power. Then give your own opinion on the nuclear energy debate.

10 Source D states that the nuclear energy industry is one of the safest industries in the world. Which Sources might be used as evidence to challenge this statement?

11 Considering all the evidence in Sources C – F , which of the following statements do you agree with?
   a Nuclear power is essential to Britain's energy needs and is a safe form of power.
   b Nuclear power is unsafe but the dangers have to be accepted because Britain needs a greater supply of energy.
   c The dangers from nuclear power are too great and Britain should develop other forms of power such as wave energy and solar energy.

12 From the evidence in the Sources C – F do you think that public concern over the use of nuclear power to generate electricity is justified or not?

13 Do you consider any of the Sources C – F to be misleading or biased? Say why, and provide examples to support your answer.

14 Can you suggest reasons which might account for people living at the same period of time holding such differing views on the use of nuclear power?

45 Britain and the Common Market

A **Extract from 'British Economic and Social History 1700–1982' by C. P. Hill, published in 1985 (Fifth edition).**
"There had been much controversy in Britain about joining. British trade with Europe had grown fast since the war, and supporters pointed to the immense potential advantages of belonging to the Common Market (as the EEC was generally called), a single free trade area containing almost 200 million people with high standards of living. Opponents preferred to stand by the established trade with the United States and the Commonwealth; they also had doubts about the effects upon certain British industries, notably agriculture, as well as about the loss of British independence of action. After failing in 1958 to become an 'associate' of the EEC rather than a full member, Britain took the lead in forming the European Free Trade Association (EFTA), consisting – in addition to herself – of Denmark, Norway, Sweden, Switzerland, Austria and Portugal.

British politicians . . . still hankered after the greater potential advantages of the EEC. After two failures (1961–3 and 1966–7), caused by the opposition of the French President, General de Gaulle, Britain was admitted to full membership in 1973. . . ."

C **Extract from a speech by President de Gaulle of France, 14 January 1963.**
"The Common Market of the Six forms a coherent whole; they have many points in common. Britain is very different. She is hardly an agricultural country at all. Also, unlike the Six, she has special political and military relations with the outside. For a long time, far from wanting to enter the Common Market, she has tried to impede its progress. Her way of buying most of her food at low prices overseas and of subsidizing her farmers is incompatible with the Common Market system. Will she accept the Common Market tariff, abandon Commonwealth preference, stop claiming privileges for her agriculture. . .? That is the real question."

D **Cartoon from 'Punch'.**

"HE SAYS HE WANTS TO JOIN—ON HIS OWN TERMS . . ."

B **Cartoon by Vicky, 1957.**

"I suspect you of driving under the influence of America."

E The front and back views of a British coin.

Questions

1 *Read Source* A .
   a Is Source A a primary or a secondary source? Explain your answer.
   b Why did some people: (i) want Britain to join the Common Market; (ii) oppose the idea of Britain joining the Common Market?
   c What was EFTA? In what ways did it differ from the EEC?
   d How many times did Britain apply for membership of the Common Market?

2 *Look at Source* B .
   a Source B shows the political leaders of France (President Charles de Gaulle (1)) and Germany (Chancellor Konrad Adenauer (2)) belonging to the same 'Club'. Was it: (i) the United Nations (UN); (ii) the Common Market (EEC); or (iii) the North Atlantic Treaty Organization (NATO)?
   b What did members of the 'Club' have to agree to accept?
   c The British Prime Minister, Harold Macmillan (3), is shown trying to join the Common Market 'on his own terms'. Are the leaders of France and Germany shown welcoming or rejecting the British Prime Minister?

3 *Read Source* C .
   Was de Gaulle in favour of Britain joining the Common Market or not?

4 *Look at Source* D . How has the cartoonist:
   (i) shown the British Prime Minister, Harold Wilson, trying to enter Europe?
   (ii) shown the French President, Charles de Gaulle, preventing Britain's entry?
   (iii) indicated the year of Britain's second attempt to join the Common Market?

5 *Look at Source* E .
   a The coin (Source E) was minted to celebrate Britain's entry into the Common Market. What is the value of the coin and in which year was it minted?
   b The 'tails' side of the coin provides historical evidence about the Common Market in 1973. What might an historian learn from studying the coin. What might an historian want to know about the coin?
   c Can you suggest why this coin differed from coins of the same value minted in other years?

Linking evidence

6 How many countries were members of the Common Market in 1963 (Source C) and 1973 (Source E)?

7 According to Sources A , B , C and D which European leader consistently opposed Britain's entry into the Common Market in the 1950s and 1960s?

8 In what ways did President de Gaulle of France believe that Britain was different from the member countries of the Common Market (Source C)? How has the cartoonist illustrated this point in Source B ?

9 Which Sources comment on the influence of the United States on Britain?

Acknowledgements

The author and publishers would like to thank the following for permission to reproduce copyright material:

B T Batsford Ltd (Taken from LIFE IN BRITAIN IN THE INTER-WAR YEARS by LCB Seaman) page 96 D; BBC Hulton Picture Library pages 24 D, 48 B, 52 A, 53 E, 78 A; Bristol University Library page 88 B; By permission of the British Library pages 13 ii, 74 A, 94 D; By permission of the British Library Newspaper Library pages 110 C, 122 B; Reproduced by Courtesy of the Trustees of the British Museum pages 44 B, 60 A, 70 A; Crown Copyright Reserved page 38 A & B; Express Newspapers page 98 C; Mary Evans Picture Library pages 18 F, 54 E, 82 B; Evening Standard/Solo pages 110 D, 116 B, C & D, 122 B; John Freeman, London pages 50 F, 60 B; By courtesy of the Trustees of the Goodwood Collections and with acknowledgements to the West Sussex Record Office and County Archivist page 12 i (WSRO Goodwood MS E30 p 57);

Illustrated London News Picture Library 82 A; Trustees of the Imperial War Museum pages 92 B, 104 A & B; Stephen Johnson page 115 C; The Hulton Picture Company pages 108 C, 112 A; Kirklees Libraries, Museums and Arts page 66 C; Manchester Public Libraries, Local History Library page 56 B; The Mansell Collection pages 20 B, 22 B, 57 C, 70 B, 74 D; Popperfoto page 100 B; Crown Copyright: Public Record Office Rail 846/98 page 36 F; Reproduced by permission of *Punch* pages 46 D, 64 D, 68 D, 72 A, 76 C, 88 C, 90 C, 96 B, 108 B, 114 A, 118 A & B, 122 D; Rochdale Local Studies Library page 100 A; Trustees of the Science Museum, London pages 16 A, 26 A, 27 D, 42 F; Sheffield City Libraries pages 80 A; University of Reading, Institute of Agricultural History and the Museum of English Rural Life page 10 C.

Index